Ocean Oracle

Ocean Oracle

What Seashells Reveal about Our True Nature

Michelle Ziff Hanson

BEYOND
WORDS
Publishing
I N C

Beyond Words Publishing, Inc.
20827 N.W. Cornell Road, Suite 500
Hillsboro, Oregon 97124-9808
503-531-8700

Editor: Jenefer Angell
Managing editor: Beth Caldwell Hoyt
Proofreader: Marvin Moore
Design: Jerry Soga
Composition: William H. Brunson Typography Services

Printed in Korea
Distributed to the book trade by Publishers Group West

Library of Congress Cataloging-in-Publication Data
Hanson, Michelle Ziff.
    Ocean oracle : what seashells reveal about our true nature / Michelle Ziff Hanson.
      p. cm.
    ISBN 1-58270-113-X (pbk.)
    1. Fortune-telling by shells.   I. Title.
BF1891.S48H36   2004
   133.3—dc22

                            2004002416

The corporate mission of Beyond Words Publishing, Inc.:
Inspire to Integrity

To Dr. R. Tucker Abbott

Although we never met, over half my personal seashell library is authored or co-authored by Dr. Abbott. I began reading his books as a child, and as my interest matured, he remained a constant companion on my bookshelf. The foundation of my seashell knowledge comes from books, and I consider Dr. Abbott to be the closest facsimile to my teacher. I am grateful for this opportunity to proclaim my appreciation for his life's work.

Dear Reader,

Welcome to the wondrous world of seashell divination!

From childhood, most of us are drawn to the whisperings of the ocean and captivated by the shapes and colors of its many treasures. Remember listening to shells as a child? Instinct was telling you they had something to say. Through seashell divination, you can listen again—and understand. It may be enough to simply delight in the beauty of shells and their mollusks (the creatures that create and inhabit shells) for all the joy they inspire, but if you listen more closely, you may also hear a deeper wisdom. Over the years I've learned to pay attention to the lessons the shells offer, and the insights I've gained have transformed my own life and the lives of many others. It is now my privilege to share this fascinating practice with you.

I love my name because it makes me one of the shells. I am the Shell with the vocal cords, and I would like to use them to introduce you to the rest of my seashell partners. Whether you use this book as a source of scientific information about seashells and mollusks, as a tool for exploring your subconscious, or as an adjunct to your own spiritual practice, in whatever capacity you decide to employ this book, you honor us.

Michelle "Shelley" Hanson

Contents

Acknowledgments

The interaction of the four basic elements of water, earth, fire, and air made this project possible.

Of these, water's influence is most apparent in seashell divination. Shells, my partners in this endeavor, have left their ocean beds and found a home with me.

My parents provided the element of earth. By naming me Michelle and calling me Shelley, they set me on my path and nurtured my obsession for information about shells and mollusks. They encouraged me to till unexplored ground in the field of metaphysics and reinforced my belief to never weed out whatever unconventional thoughts may sprout without first examining their worth. They motivated me to harvest what I could from my studies and inspirations. My mother keeps a list of my shell inventory on hand wherever she travels, intent on finding new members to join my seashell family. My father assisted me in designing promotional materials and gifted me with a microphone, which literally gives me a voice when I speak at seminars. The guidance and support of my exceptional parents allowed my love of shells to bloom and flourish. Without them, this book would not exist.

I am eternally grateful to my friend Robert Wendler for first suggesting that I try seashell reading. But that initial spark—the fire—that told me I could read meanings in shells would have flickered and died out were it not for my passionate husband, Don, the love of my life. Lovingly blending his strength with mine, the fragile, tiny spark became a glowing flame. His active support and enduring love gave me the courage to share this idea with others.

My family and friends have added air to this equation, fanning the flame into a roaring fire. I thank all those who allowed me to interpret shells for them, in turn further strengthening my conviction in the language of seashells. Their inspiring suggestions added to the other intangible wisps with which I began to form something material—most notably, this book. Were it not for my loved ones continuously breathing new life into my desire to share this information, I might have become complacent. Whether it led to introducing me to the media or to new clients, or just sharing their delight in the experience, their reactions have never failed to redouble my dedication.

Thus, this book became possible with each of the elements playing a role in my life. I am blessed beyond measure to be the recipient of so much love and support. May each of you reading this book bask in the warmth of this fire, and may its light banish the shadows to bring clarity into your life.

Introduction

The word *oracle* means a "source of wise counsel." In *Ocean Oracle*, seashells serve as the tool to reveal hidden thoughts, beliefs, and attitudes you hold that may be having an impact on your present life. You, yourself, are the source of the wisdom uncovered through use of the shells. Your own consciousness contains the know-how to overcome limitations and obstacles, and becoming aware of them provides opportunities for change. In this way, information from the shells stimulates that awareness so, if you choose, you can alter the direction of your life.

The book you hold in your hands is the culmination of a lifelong quest for information, first about shells and then about the depths of awareness. Having never lived near the ocean, my first exposure to seashells came courtesy of my grandparents. Upon returning from a vacation in Florida, they gifted their four-year-old granddaughter with shells they had gathered off the beach. Even at that young age I was famously curious among my family, and these wonders of nature inspired my curiosity with a new intensity

When I was eight years old, with my interest in shells growing ever stronger, my parents bought me Donald F. Low's *The How and Why Wonder Book of Sea Shells*. Before I was nine, I had devoured its contents from cover to cover. I was obsessed with not only the shells but the animals who create and inhabit these calcified works of art. The scientific name for these animals is *mollusk*, derived from the Latin word meaning "soft."

Mollusks are invertebrates; in other words, they lack an internal skeleton. Their shells serve as an external source of structure and support. I learned that some mollusks, such as the octopus, can exist without a shell, but no shell could exist without some mollusk having previously created it.

Not satisfied with merely memorizing the answers to the questions in Low's book, I decided to start a journal about shells. It wasn't long before anything relating to shells became fair game for my journal. I cut out newspaper and magazine articles as well as pictures from childhood coloring books. One day, while visiting my aunt, I became transfixed by her new shower curtain. The pink plastic shells were crying out to be included in my journal. Remarkably, my aunt not only allowed me to cut up her shower curtain, but she assisted me in securing the plastic shells to the pages of my precious journal.

Fortunately, my interests became less destructive. I soon discovered the world of library books and diligently copied each new piece of information into my journal. One of the first things my studies taught me was that, because there were so many thousands of species of shells, scientists divide them into five classes. I soon became determined to obtain representatives from each class. My grandparents' presents covered two classes: *univalves* (what you may picture as a typical snail shell) and *bivalves* (paired shells such as clams, oysters, and scallops). Three classes remained: *tusk shells* (resembling elephant tusks in appearance), *chitons* (the least-evolved mollusks with shells consisting of eight overlapping plates), and *cephalopods* (literally "head-foot," referring to squid, octopus, and cuttlefish, whose tentacles seem to grow from their heads).

It took years, but thanks to my family I completed my mission, finally gaining a full collection that includes shells from every class. I continued to learn everything I could about them, but at the same time my childhood habit of asking "Why?" about everything led me to delve into new areas of study. On my bookshelves, metaphysical books began to share space with my seashell books.

As my interest in metaphysics increased, so did my circle of friends and acquaintances involved in psychic exploration. One day, one of these acquaintances, Robert Wendler, spotted my seashell collection at my apartment and mentioned that he knew someone who did seashell readings. Fireworks exploded in my head. What a concept! It seemed to be the perfect marriage of my two interests. I wanted to make an appointment immediately, and Robert promised he would get me the contact information. To my disappointment, he was unable to find it. Sensing my frustration, he asked me, "Why don't you use your own shells?" I had my doubts, but I decided to give it a try. By then, I had over two hundred shells in my collection. Calling upon what I had spent my life memorizing—the name of the shell, the anatomy and behavior of the mollusk, or their interaction with humans—by the end of the week I knew what every one of those shells meant in relation to people's lives. My precious journal now had a purpose.

Despite my exploration into the metaphysical, as a scientist, I did not make the leap into seashell divination easily. I needed demonstrable proof for every meaning assigned to a shell. I felt a responsibility not only to interpret *what* the shells meant but to explain *why*.

In my search, I found four sources for deriving meanings. Based on these sources, I created four categories of shells: Behavior, Interaction, Name and Appearance, and Intuition. The meanings in the first group, Behavior, are derived from the behavior or anatomy of the mollusks. In the second, Interaction, they come from the shells' interaction with humans. In the third group, Name and Appearance, they are based on the shells' name and appearance. And lastly, the meanings of the Intuition group are based on intuition or intention.

A month later, on another visit, Robert took me aside to ask if I had considered using my shells to do readings. Although I was sure I had figured out their meanings, I hadn't progressed beyond this. Fearing criticism, I hadn't mentioned this experiment to anyone, not even my family. When Robert asked if I would read for him, however, I nervously replied that I would be willing to try. He walked over to my collection and selected two shells. My heart sank. With two hundred shells to choose from, he had chosen only two. Robert was practically a stranger to me, and what could I tell him with just two shells? I saw that one shell, the Episcopal Miter, meant religion. The other shell indicated someone going in circles and getting nowhere. I shakily gave my first seashell reading: "I don't know why, Robert, but if you are focused on religion, it looks like you might be stuck in a rut, spinning your wheels and getting nowhere." A startled expression crossed his features, followed by a beaming smile. Then he informed me that he was a former seminary student. His attraction to a combination of shells revealing his religious struggle left no doubt that it was possible to use shells for readings. I was hooked; there was no turning back.

For twelve years, I restricted my readings to family members and close friends, gaining valuable practice with my shells. I also began collecting with a new agenda. In my research, I discovered shells with meanings I wanted available for readings. My seashell wish list, formerly based on external beauty, began to reflect shells needed for their contribution to my seashell vocabulary. To accommodate this broadened vocabulary, my shell collection expanded, eventually representing over four hundred shells from all over the world. Two hundred of them are featured here for your enjoyment.

The *Ocean Oracle* set includes this book, four overview plates, and the shell cards. Here's the short version of how it works: To aid you in your reading, each of the four groups may be viewed at a glance using the enclosed overview plates. They allow you to see all the shells in the collection easily, and from this perspective you select those shells that grab your attention as most attractive or those that most repulse you. The corresponding cards are then retrieved and arranged in whatever order feels right to you before they are turned over to reveal the meanings. Later chapters contain more specific instructions for setting up and interpreting readings, sample readings, and expanded explanations for each shell's meaning.

Each of the four groups of meanings is sequenced according to how strongly its explanations are rooted in science. Since I began seashell reading still possessing a scientist's mind-set, I originally felt most confident if the meaning was based on the behavior and anatomy of the mollusk. I was also comfortable if the meaning was derived from mankind's inventive uses for shells and their inhabitants, such as money, tools, and medicine, or as a source of religious, artistic, or scientific inspiration.

I was less sure about the meanings I had ascribed to the shells based on the shell's name, because connotations from names are more subjective, but I felt confident enough that I began working with these three groups of meanings for seashell divination. The fourth group came to me much later in my career. I learned that the most important qualification for a shell's meaning is not what I can point to in a book at all. It is the intention we give it. In my work, I have found that once a meaning is set for a particular shell, it doesn't matter from where the meaning is derived. Scientific evidence can be used to corroborate meanings, but the intention supercedes everything.

Because I still possess the mind of a scientist, I must point out a few technicalities. This book is titled *Ocean Oracle: What Seashells Reveal about Our True Nature*; however, not all shells come from the sea. In one class, the univalves, species can be found in land habitats. These mollusks breathe through lungs, not gills. Some land snails appear in the section in which meanings are based on the behavior of the mollusk. In addition, some of the animals discussed, although ocean inhabitants, are not mollusks at all. Starfish, sea urchins, and sand dollars are echinoderms. They, along with sea horses and coral, are included because they live in close proximity to mollusks and their behaviors add to this vocabulary.

When word of my seashell reading spread, I received invitations to do readings at psychic fairs. To prevent damaging my shells while traveling to these venues, I photographed them. I discovered that the photographs served well as substitutes. Satisfied that the subconscious message can still be revealed through photographs, I now offer this oracle set so you may experience this extraordinary gift yourself. Mother Nature has so much to teach us, if we are willing to listen.

The following pages contain what I call the language of the shells. To help you as you develop your own interpretation skills, I have included snippets of past readings that represent a broad spectrum of what I have witnessed. I hope you will look upon what the shells have taught me as an indicator of what they may hold in store for you.

PART ONE
THE SOURCE OF MEANINGS

Behavior Group:
Meanings Based on the Behavior and
Anatomy of the Mollusk

As mentioned in the introduction, the meanings in this group are strongly rooted in science. Your attraction to shells in this group will relate to the animal's particular behavior and anatomy.

A shell surrounds a mollusk's body the way an article of clothing such as a shirt surrounds a person. Imagine that we each emerge as babies with a shirt that fits us perfectly. The shirt remains with us throughout our life, and as our bodies grow, we must continuously add material so it will continue to fit our new dimensions. Now, if someone collects shirts, he or she may have a diverse collection of different sizes, colors, and patterns, but these variations do not reflect the variation in physical anatomy and behavior of the people who inhabit them. Similarly, in this category of meanings the point of attraction may be a clam shell, but its meaning comes from the behavior of the clam mollusk that made it. Take, for example, the Angel Wing clam mollusk, which makes the Angel Wing clam shell. The Angel Wing clam mollusk is the only mollusk that entombs itself for protection. If necessary, it can bore through rock. The excavation takes a long time, and this unique behavior lends the meaning to its shell, represented here as determination.

The study of mollusks (malacology) has taught me that the many varieties of these animals have very little in common. Aside from the obvious differences in appearance, color, pattern, shape, and size, mollusks are also vastly different in terms of location, eating habits, anatomy, reproduction, locomotion, and protection. Mollusks can dwell on the deepest ocean bottoms, or in the case of land snails, they may be found on mountain peaks. They can endure equatorial heat or live in the arctic. They range from filter feeders to vegetarians to carnivores. Some are even cannibals.

In all my research, I have found only two things mollusks have in common with each other: a mantle (the body tissue that secretes the shell) and a foot—a single foot. (Even the tentacles of the octopus are formed from one foot that subdivided during their evolution.) Other than these two body parts, I have found nothing else that all mollusks share. While most mollusks have shells, for example, there are still exceptions, such as the octopus, which possesses a mantle but has long since lost the shell that fossil evidence reveals its ancestors produced. Similarly, while almost every mollusk's blood is blue or clear, using copper to carry the oxygen, the Blood Ark and the Bittersweet clams defy this trait by having red blood. (They use iron-based hemoglobin, a much more efficient oxygen carrier and an advantage in oxygen-depleted environments.)

To aid in identification, scientists have divided the estimated one hundred thousand species of shells into six classes. One of these classes, the monoplacophora, was considered extinct until a few "living fossils" were discovered in the 1950s. Since shells of this primitive class are extremely rare, we will focus on the five classes mentioned previously: univalves, bivalves, tusk shells, chitons, and cephalopods.

Still, when considering the mollusks responsible for producing these shells, within the individual classes tremendous diversity exists. Most mollusks have gills and require a water habitat, but some univalves, the land snails, live on land and breathe through lungs. Mollusks sometimes lack either a head or centralized brain. Some have no eyes, while scallops have nearly a hundred eyes. Some have poor vision, while the octopus can see you as clearly as you see him. The octopus also has three separate hearts, each comprising a single chamber. Two of the hearts obtain oxygen from the gills, and the other supplies blood to the rest of the body. This abundance of hearts is a dramatic contrast to the anatomy found in tusk mollusks. Some texts claim that tusks have no heart, theorizing that their foot muscle contracts to pump blood. Newer texts suggest that tusks may possess a very primitive heart organ. The most-evolved molluscan hearts belong to the clam. Although they have no head, clams have a three-chambered heart with a pacemaker setting its rhythm, an arrangement very similar to our own.

Reproduction is likewise varied. Bivalves tend to release huge quantities of sperm and eggs into the ocean, making fertilization a random process. Through heterosexual mating, some mollusks are capable of forming egg cases where the young hatch and eventually form a shell; other mollusks have their shell intact upon hatching. Some mollusks bear live young. Some are hermaphrodites, with both male and female sex organs, and can perform both roles for each other. Yet other mollusks begin life as a male member of a colony and, as hormone levels change in the colony, become female.

Mollusk methods of locomotion also run the gamut. An adult giant clam weighing in at five hundred pounds leads a sedentary life. Other mollusks can crawl, jump, or swim rapidly by jet propulsion. One mollusk, the Janthina, is unable to swim yet dwells far from shore on the surface of the ocean. It accomplishes this by floating on a homemade raft of mucus-cemented air bubbles.

Mollusks have a variety of fascinating methods to protect themselves. They may employ camouflage, anesthetics, or poison. They may live in harsh climates to limit competition or attack head-on with ferocity. Some have very short life spans, while others lengthen their existence by regenerating parts such as a foot or an eye.

These are just a sampling of the differences in mollusks' anatomy and behaviors. The shells produced by these mollusks derive their meanings from each animal's unique qualities. Their many variations lend even more significance to readings because the meanings of several shells may also be considered together, and these interrelationships provide endless possibilities for interpretation.

Interaction Group:
Meanings Based on the Interaction with Humans

In central France, a family of cavemen was found buried with seashell necklaces. It is surmised that the shells came from cavemen living near the coast and were traded several times to make their way inland to where they were found buried.

This discovery gives eloquent testimony to the value that humans have placed on shells since they first walked the Earth. Throughout history, humans have found multiple uses for shells and mollusks. The meanings in this group are derived from our relationships with shells and mollusks developed over millennia and still playing out today. The word *purple*, for example, comes directly from the Purpura Murex, a shellfish that was the source for the purple dye coveted by ancient aristocracy and used almost exclusively to color royal garments. Similarly, cowrie shells gave us the word *porcelain*. During the Roman Empire, cowries were known as *porcellana*, meaning "little pig," because their puckered openings resemble certain anatomy of female pigs. When fine pottery was introduced to European society from the Far East, the polished surface of these new items reminded people of the porcellana shells, and the term *porcelain* was given to the pottery.

Ancient Egyptians believed that small cowrie shells (the underside of which, when held horizontally, resembles an eye) placed in a mummy's eye sockets would provide vision in the afterlife. Polynesians do the same to decorate the eyes of their idols. In one Japanese tradition, women believed that holding a particular shell during labor would ease childbirth. Shells have been employed in mundane practical applications as tools. They have also served as inspiration for artists, jewelers, musicians, and architects. Scallops signify ancestral heroism in British coats of arms. In India, chank shells represent a connection to Vishnu and symbolize religious adoration. Shells provided one of man's earliest means of monetary exchange, eventually leading to the concept of coins as currency.

Mollusks have also been valuable to us in a variety of ways. For some, they simply provide a nutritious meal. Others extol the aphrodisiac qualities they claim oysters confer. Scientists recognize their medicinal potential. Extracts from various mollusks have aided in fighting afflictions from headaches and the common cold to more serious bacterial infections and tremors. Some extracts from mollusks have been found to have antiviral properties and may even inhibit cancer growth. Studying the capacity of various drugs to block reception of the clams' natural pacemaker signal has yielded valuable insights for our own heart health. Sepia ink and the principle behind the operation of the submarine were both derived from observing mollusks.

While the meanings in this group are well-established, there is fertile ground for expansion as human imagination finds new values for shells and mollusks.

Name and Appearance Group: Meanings Based on the Name and Appearance of the Shell

The meanings in this group are often more easily recognizable than in the others, as they are based on name, appearance, or both. For example, once you are aware a particular bivalve is called the Wedding Cake Venus Clam and see the cake-like tiers of its shape, you may understand why its meaning relates to weddings, marriage, or a committed relationship. Another is the Giant Sundial shell, which reminded its discoverer of ancient sundials used to track the passage of time. The meaning for this one refers to a need for patience, a necessary quality when one finds the slow passage of time difficult to endure.

As you become acquainted with the meanings of the shells in this group, you may find yourself sometimes agreeing with the names and other times asking yourself, "What possessed someone to give this shell that name?" Note that the meaning is based on the name given to the shell without taking its suitability into account.

The first person to discover a new species of shell is granted the privilege of naming it. The shell's name is then transferred to the mollusk that created it. The clam mollusk inhabits a clam shell, just as an oyster mollusk creates its oyster shell. As with every living organism, each shell has a common name (in English) and a scientific name (in Latin) that designates both genus and species. For example, shells bearing the names Watering Pot, Wedding Cake Venus Clam, Giant Sundial, and Cat's Tongue Oyster are known by the scientific community as *Brechites attrahens*, *Callanaitis disjecta*, *Architectonica maxima*, and *Spondylus linguaefelis*, respectively. Latin binomials ensure that people from any country or field of study can precisely specify the organism in question, which prevents the confusion that can arise over variations in an animal's common name. Personally, I have always related more easily to the vivid descriptive qualities in common names, so these are what I used to derive the meanings in this section, unless otherwise indicated.

Intuition Group:
Meanings Based on Intuition

Since childhood, I have sought scientific explanations for life's mysteries. As an adult, this trait applies to my seashell readings as well. I was only comfortable if each designated meaning could be traced to some passage in a scientific text. As the previous sections have shown, using the mollusk's anatomy or behavior or its interaction with man, or simply the shell's name or appearance, allowed me to point to supportive, documented evidence.

This self-imposed requirement for scientific confirmation was literally shattered when one of my shells was broken. I was forced to use an unrelated species as a stand-in for the meaning represented by the broken shell. My belief was put to the test when my client selected the substitute shell. Although this shell technically meant something entirely different, I used the meaning assigned to the broken shell it had replaced. To my surprise, this resulted in a most insightful reading, and it aided my client in uncovering and healing some issues held deep in denial. This success taught me a valuable lesson. After all those years, I discovered that it doesn't matter if I have scientific evidence confirming a shell's meaning. All that matters is the intended meaning I give it—and the wisdom looking to make its way out takes over from there.

The last section of this book is devoted to meanings obtained through this realization. At times, I had a meaning in mind first and then chose a shell to represent it. Other times, I simply meditated with a shell to discover what it had to teach. Quite unexpectedly, something wonderful happened. By relinquishing the need to seek scientific corroboration, I began to receive it—long after I had established a shell's meaning. In these cases, the process essentially worked in reverse.

My discovery of the Marble Cone shell's meaning is one example of this. For years, based on my own intuition, I felt that this shell represented ruin and disappointment. Years later, I read an account of the Dutch artist Rembrandt, who was commissioned to make an etching of the Marble Cone. Ironically, his etching of the very shell that means ruin and disappointment was itself ruined. Based on this documented interaction with Rembrandt, the discussion of the Marble Cone appears in the Interaction Group rather than the Intuition Group as it would have before I made this discovery. Over the years, as I continue to increase my knowledge, other shells have made the transition from this final section to those I consider more proven. This renews my confidence when considering what the next unknown shell may have to say.

So, the shells in this section have no documented reason for their meaning—yet. However, they serve my clients equally as well as those for which I do have scientific confirmation. The key is to establish a clear intention for a shell to have a particular meaning prior to a reading. I mention this because, if you are so inclined, you can use any of these shells to develop your own meanings. As you become comfortable with the shells, allow them to speak to you. You may feel guided to fine-tune or alter some of the meanings I use. Seashell readings are living things, constantly evolving as new shells and clients come into my life. Some I seek out, some find me. All are valuable contributors to this work in progress. The shells and I invite you to join in the conversation.

PART TWO
YOUR TURN

Instructions for
Using the Ocean Oracle

Before you begin your own readings, let's address a few questions:

Who can perform readings? Readings can be performed by an individual for him or herself, or someone else can perform a reading for you. Both approaches are discussed later in this section.

How often should you have a reading? This is entirely up to you. The shells are ready to work with you any time you seek guidance. As a general rule of thumb, I suggest that clients wait a few months between readings to allow time for absorbing the information and altering any behaviors they choose to transform. However, any time circumstances change in your life, or clarity is needed, the shells are here to assist you.

How does shell divination work? If you enter a room with the television and radio turned off, the airwaves still contain news broadcasts. You may be oblivious to this and unable to "tune in" to the information until you physically turn on the television or radio to assist your reception. In the same way, our energy broadcasts volumes of information about us, but not all of us are "turned on" to receive. The shells function as tools to assist us in receiving the broadcast from our inner self, just as turning on the television allows us to become aware of the news floating through the air currents surrounding us. The following steps will guide you to using the shells to receive their information:

1. Quiet your mind.

When reading for yourself: To prepare for a reading, take a moment to close your eyes and empty your mind of distracting thoughts. Breathe deeply. Sometimes, repeating something silently to yourself, such as your name, aids in quieting the chatter so you can clear your mind. If you find too many thoughts creeping back in, politely redirect your attention to your breath or your name or whatever you have chosen to help calm you. When you are ready, using the name on your birth certificate, repeat your first name a few times to yourself before opening your eyes. *Note:* A rabbi once told me that your name on your birth certificate is the closest thing to pure prophecy because it is your essence, your soul's vibration. The purpose here is to connect with your higher self and to avoid involving your personality.

When reading for another: Silently ask your higher self to join with the higher selves of both the shells themselves and the person for whom you are reading. As you form this partnership, ask to be a clear and accurate messenger of the information, and ask for it to be obtained for the client's highest good.

In either case, when a person suddenly thinks that a certain shell is pretty—or repulsive—it is because their higher self has a message to reveal through this shell. The reader's job is simply to convey or translate the message based on the arrangement of the shells. Using this book, people can cut out the middleman. The key is to keep personalities out of the equation.

2. Be open to the message that your higher self wants you to know.

The subconscious will often deliver whatever message it considers most important. Only after it has the chance to deliver this message will it move to another topic. You may find that your subconscious has very different priorities than your conscious self, and the shells allow it to speak without your interference.

You may also focus on a specific question before you pick shells, but be aware that regardless of the question you want to address, the message from your higher self will be delivered first.

3. Choose your shells.

Open your eyes and spread the overview plates in front of you. Look at both the front and the back of each plate. Observe which shells jump out at you. Don't question why, but note the particular number assigned to shells you find attractive as well as to those that repulse you.

Using the number on the overview-plate photo, retrieve the matching card and set it aside. The color rectangles at the top of each plate correspond to the color outlines on the back of each card. Repeat this process of discovering what shells jump out at you on the overview plates, noting their numbers, and retrieving the individual shell cards. Alternatively, simply record the numbers designating all the shells you want to use, and once finished with the selection process, retrieve the cards matching your list.

The number of cards selected should not be limited. If a shell stands out for any reason, it should be included in the reading regardless of your reaction to it. You may admire it, be repulsed by it, or even feel indifferent. If it claims your attention, it counts. When all the remaining shells seem to blend together, with nothing claiming your attention, you are done.

Note: If looking at the overview photographs becomes overwhelming, or when you become so familiar with the shells' meanings that you can't pick objectively, you can also proceed without viewing the pictures on the plates or cards. Using the individual cards, close your eyes, empty your mind, and allow yourself to pull out as many cards as you feel you should, sight unseen. Once you have your selection, open your eyes and separate out any cards you don't like. This method allows the subconscious to speak just as clearly.

4. Arrange your shells.

Once you have collected all the individual cards of the shells that appeal to you, place them in an arrangement. There is no right or wrong way to do this. They may all form one group or be separated into any design that you find attractive.

5. Read meanings.

When you are satisfied with your arrangement, simply turn over the shell cards to reveal their meanings. In addition to the abbreviated meanings on the back, you may also refer to the more detailed corresponding explanations in this book—though it isn't necessary to know why a shell has a particular meaning.

If there are any shells you don't like, turn these over too. These refer to issues of denial or something that you prefer not to confront. If you find yourself feeling indifferent to certain shells, these are beliefs in transition. You may recognize that they no longer serve you but hesitate to embrace a new belief to replace it. See the next section on interpretation for more on how to use these cards.

6. Interpret the message.

The shells may be likened to vocabulary words: their arrangement determines the sequence for stringing the words into sentences and paragraphs. Stringing together the meanings, relating them to each other based on the pattern of your arrangement, makes the communication from your inner self more pointed.

To illustrate, think of the shells as vocabulary words. Suppose you had these ten words:

dog, boy, girl, the, chased, a, with, and, played, some

You could arrange these words any number of ways:

The dog chased a boy and played with some girl.
The boy played with some dog and chased a girl.

Using exactly the same words, these two different arrangements convey two very different messages. You could select the same ten shells as someone else, but your arrangements might be so different that the message is completely different too. What matters is what you put next to each other. Please refer to the sample readings for more clarification on the value of arrangement.

Keys to Interpretation

Remember what you are looking for. Keep in mind that the point of a reading is to allow you the opportunity to discover the beliefs and attitudes you hold that may no longer serve you. With awareness, we have choice.

The shells you choose, whether you are drawn to them or dislike them, are delivering a message from your subconscious. Once you have all the meanings in relationship to each other from your design, you have your message. When interpreting the message, remember that these thoughts are currently having an impact on your life even if you aren't consciously aware of them.

If further clarification is needed, hold the picture of the shell you would like more information about. Now focus on this one shell and look again at the overview plates. This time, pick shells that you feel "go" with this picture, and also pay attention to any new shells that you notice you do not like.

Shells that repulse you may still have a positive message. Don't be surprised if, at first glance, the meanings associated with the shells you dislike don't seem to apply to you. Often, the qualities represented in the dislike area are the way you consciously live your life. For instance, someone may "dislike" shells representing altruism or generosity—which does *not* mean that she is a selfish or stingy person. The shells are saying that, for whatever reason, she really doesn't like giving as much as she may think she does. With honest exploration from selecting more shells, she may discover that her generosity has backfired. She may harbor feelings that her efforts are unappreciated. Possibly she feels overwhelmed by what she or others expect of her. Perhaps giving to others prohibits devoting quality time to herself. Revealing these hidden thoughts may allow her to change unhelpful life patterns so that she may properly satisfy her own needs and give to others more joyfully.

Your eyes will see only the shells you need. You are a work in progress, and you will see the shells you require as the need arises. You may also find that a shell will no longer repulse you when the issue it refers to is brought to your awareness and healed.

I often have clients ask if a shell they hadn't seen on a previous visit is new. It never is; they simply didn't notice it until the issues associated with it became relevant. In fact, my shell collection is displayed in two tall cabinets with six shelves each. If a shell applies to a client's need, it can be on the top shelf and the client will see it, while those shells at eye level are overlooked. For this reason, I long ago ceased feeling the need to rotate the shells.

Get out of the way of the message. When the shells' meanings don't seem immediately relevant, it's typical for the mind to interfere by casting doubt. It is important to always stay true to the shells' meanings without attempting to alter the message in some way that makes it seem a better fit.

During the time when I was still only reading for family and close friends, one particular experience taught me to let the shells speak without interference. While employed as a medical technician at a local hospital, I discovered that a new friend at work shared my love of seashells. When I told her that shells could be used to do readings, she couldn't wait to have her shells read. During her reading, she selected two egg cases, both denoting birth. As I revealed this, I was acutely aware that my friend, only recently married, had no desire to become pregnant so soon. I informed her that she was probably on the verge of a great spiritual birth.

A week later, while I was eating in the hospital cafeteria, my friend spotted me across the room and yelled, "Hey, Shelley, remember that reading you did for me?" Embarrassed at the attention, I nodded yes. Then she asked, "Remember what it was about?" Hoping to end the conversation, I mumbled one word: *birth*. Suddenly, as if controlled by a master puppeteer, the mouths of everyone with her dropped open in unison. She had just received lab results indicating that she was pregnant. The shells had revealed this information a week ago, but I let myself second-guess and interfere with the interpretation. This experience left an indelible impression on me. I resolved to get out of the way when delivering a message. Ever since, my policy has been to state whatever the shells say without judging how the message may be received.

Trust that the shells know what they are doing. I'd like to share several experiences that taught me to always trust what the shells have to say:

Mary

After maintaining a low profile for twelve years, I gave my first reading for a stranger. Mary selected ten shells that she liked and four shells she didn't. Combined, they revealed a deceitful loved one, a con artist, which upset her greatly. Concerned about her emotional state, I spent a restless night hoping the information we discussed would prove helpful to her.

The next day, another woman called, stating that Mary had referred her to me. I was relieved that Mary, despite her tears, must have felt the shell reading had been of some value to her.

As the new caller selected her shells, I noticed she was drawn to seven of the same shells Mary had used. She arranged her shells in a figure eight, and those seven emotion-laden shells comprised half of the figure eight. There was the same distressing tale of a deceitful loved one. With over four hundred shells to choose from, I wondered how these same shells could appear twice in two days. Something had to be wrong. Because these were my first two readings for strangers, I wondered if I had deluded myself regarding seashell reading. Was it possible that I had influenced all previous readings in some way?

The figure eight seemed to be divided into separate arenas: half career and half home. The seven identical shells were part of the home section. I asked how this client knew Mary. She smiled and told me she would tell me later. Attempting to preserve a professional demeanor, I asked her if any shells repulsed her in some way, and I lost all composure as she pointed to the same four shells that Mary had noticed the day before. I considered the possibility that Mary had told her which shells she didn't like. However, I found no quality these four shells shared. They were different colors and shapes and were even located on different shelves in my cabinet. There was simply no way Mary could have guided her to pick these identical shells.

At a loss, I had to halt the reading until I could ascertain how this client knew Mary. She calmly informed me that Mary was her mother. She didn't seem surprised at all by my revelation that her shells were identical to her mother's. However, by my calculations, with four hundred seashells, the odds that two members of the same family would be drawn to the same shells had to be astronomical. Since this reading, I have witnessed family members repeat this feat three other times, and I have often seen family members selecting one or two of the same pivotal shells in their readings.

With the shells' repetitive insistence now explained, my original position of doubt and concern that something was wrong dramatically transformed into a wellspring of trust that the shells know what they are doing.

Edith

Another experience that reinforced this lesson came from Edith, a grandmother who came to me with a question she wanted answered.

To ensure that my interpretation remained free from bias, I requested that she select the shells without informing me of her question. Before I began my interpretation, I surveyed her arrangement and noted that the shells she selected stated that what came easily in the past would now require hard work. They suggested the need for balancing Eastern wisdom with Western, intuition with logic. They informed her that help was available but that her pride prevented her from asking for it. They indicated that a present sacrifice would lead to a future reward. The focus of everything centered around, of all things, school. I must admit, looking at this woman who could be my grandmother, I had my doubts as I told her what the shells were saying.

I was delighted to discover that the shells did answer her question. She told me she was sixty-nine and starting a four-year college course. As a former Harvard graduate with no scholastic problems, she now had great difficulty outlining information and using the computer. She had been an artist for several years, and the logical side of her brain had lain dormant. She understood why the shells indicated that she needed to sacrifice her pride to ask for help. This present sacrifice held the potential for a future reward.

Linda

The last and by far the most powerful illustration of trusting the shells came from a reading I once gave to a woman named Linda, who selected several shells regarding abuse and violation, a combination I had never seen before. As I began the interpretation, Linda reacted as if it had no connection to her at all. At this stage in my career, I trusted that the shells were accurate, but I knew that my interpretation could be wrong. To aid me in clarifying what I was seeing, I asked her to select more shells. As each shell confirmed the previous message and added more details, her denial became more adamant. I was at a loss to explain how my interpretation could be so wrong. After an hour of denial, she broke down. In a barely audible voice, she proceeded to sketch a nightmarish tale of abuse from her father and by her husband. Terrified upon hearing her own words, she whispered, "Nobody knows this, not even the friends I came with. How do the shells know?"

I explained that the shells are tools used by the subconscious. In effect, she was having a conversation with herself, and my role, as the interpreter, was to assist her in gaining awareness of the burden she was carrying. Even feelings held in deep denial color behavior and can be responsible for creating repetitious and harmful life patterns.

Wishing to curtail her suffering, I asked only one more question. She responded by mutely pointing to seashells. The shells she fingered spoke volumes, which I stated aloud.

Nodding her head, she acknowledged them as an accurate reflection of her thoughts. Using this technique, we were able to continue the conversation without requiring her to continue speaking the details herself.

The reading allowed her to excavate these feelings to assist her in healing. The shells coaxed her to confront her nightmare while sparing her the pain of speaking the words aloud. Taking her first shaky steps out of darkness, she ended the session by stating her willingness to schedule an appointment with a therapist. Previously paralyzed for years by shame and fear, this step wouldn't even have been possible prior to her reading.

This reading, more than any prior or since, taught me the degree to which the shells can assist us. I include myself in that "us" for two reasons. First, although she had denied the message for an hour, I had learned to trust the shells. My persistence was eventually rewarded with her confession, leading to the beginning of an opportunity for her to heal. Second, the gift I received witnessing her speaking through the shells clearly demonstrated that this is a language available to everyone.

Your inner self holds all the answers. If you follow the steps above, the shells will help you tap into your own wisdom. Different methods work better for certain issues, so if you are having difficulty getting a clear reading, keep experimenting. I sometimes use photographs when working with clients, even if the client is in my home and has access to the real shells. I've also found that the deeper the issue, the greater the need to work without looking at the shells before choosing, as this eliminates the conscious desire to control the message. The key in every instance is to remain open to what the shells have to say. After all, this is a message from your inner self, and who knows you better? It knows every private wound you have buried or forgotten, every event that led to a belief about you and the world. I leave you now in good hands as the shells aid you in a conversation with your best friend—your inner self.

Sample Readings

The following pages are designed to demonstrate the steps involved in performing and interpreting a reading. In the first example, the reader has chosen eight seashells that she liked from the overview plates—placed in two separate arrangements—and three she disliked. The corresponding shell cards are retrieved by matching the number on the overview plates to the number appearing beneath the picture of the shell on its card.

The cards are placed picture-side up in any arrangement found to be pleasing. Turning over the shell cards reveals their individual meanings. It then becomes a matter of stringing the meanings together based on their relationship in the arrangement.

Using the shell's assigned number, the reader can employ this book to find more details regarding the shell's meaning and an explanation for its derivation.

Like

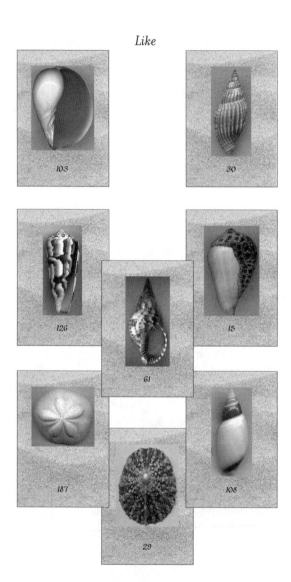

Dislike

Turning the cards over, the reader can now begin to understand what these cards mean.

With these two cards, the subconscious message is that *the relationship the reader is in has created trouble*. This is perceived as unhealthy, and she is encouraged to *bail out* of this relationship.

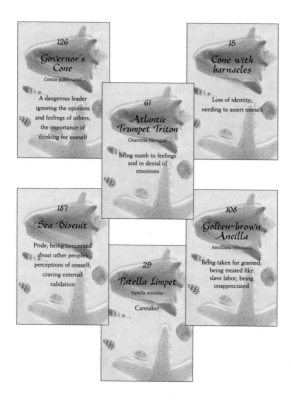

This group of shells reveals the central issue that this person is *unaware of her feelings*. The fact that the cards were laid out touching each other indicates that these issues are connected. Although this person *takes care of others*, she won't allow herself to recognize that this *goes unappreciated*. She won't acknowledge hurt *pride*. She won't let herself recognize that her *feelings and opinions are discounted*. The subconscious warns that by continuing in this relationship, the client is in danger of *losing her iden-*

tity. All of this is repressed consciously as the client *numbs her feelings*.

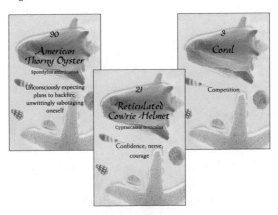

Now let's look at the shells that were disliked. These are issues in denial or things that this person doesn't want to confront. She dislikes *competition*. She lacks *confidence*, possibly because her *actions have backfired* in the past.

From this we can gain some understanding of why this person would remain in—and may be unaware of—an unhealthy relationship where she isn't appreciated. Fear of competition would discourage her from returning to square one in the dating world, as would lack of confidence. *It may seem preferable to remain in an unhealthy relationship and to numb her recognition of this because she feels incapable of confidently facing the competition of dating again.*

The value of arrangement may be more clearly demonstrated in the following examples. We will use the same two shells in each example and see how the interpretation varies based on their placement:

Shell	Name	Meaning
6	Sunburst Carrier	Preferring to be alone; avoiding attachments
35	Nassa Snail	Believing that the ends justify the means

Like
6
35

Liking both shells says that you like to be alone and that you believe the ends justify the means. You will do whatever is required to preserve your solitude. This may entail pushing others away, taking the phone off the hook, or even acting rude to discourage others from invading your time.

Dislike
6
35

Disliking both shells says that even though you don't like to be alone, you are not willing to do whatever it takes to avoid loneliness. If you don't enjoy someone's company or don't care for the activity planned, you will not go. There are some things you will not do if the discomfort outweighs the benefit of the companionship.

Dislike   Like
35   6

This combination says that you treasure solitude but that there are some things you will not do in pursuit of your time alone. You will not be rude, avoid phone calls, or ignore others.

Dislike   **Like**
6   35
This combination says that you do not like being alone and
that you will do whatever is necessary, including putting up
with anything or anyone, just to have company.

PART THREE
CARD EXPLANATIONS AND MEANINGS

As you get familiar with the explanations and meanings, you may notice that not all the meanings are expressed in the same form. For example, sometimes a meaning can be a simple concept (such as *Competition*), a more comprehensive concept (such as *Blowing things out of proportion*), or even a person (such as *A good friend*). While I have endeavored to make them as consistent as possible, the nature of the material prevents me from imposing a rigid form on the meanings that could potentially distort a reading.

I have also resisted the temptation to limit the meanings of the cards to only those that I have seen most commonly in my work. For example, the Solander's Trivia shell (no. 161) generally means *Trivial, unimportant*. While I see this most often applied to people's feelings about their lives, as I note in the explanation, the concept of trivia is so broad that a person could conceivably be drawn to the shell for various reasons. The only certainty is that it will relate to trivia in some way.

It is important to remember that unless a person is attracted only to a single card, the significance of a card's meaning is always affected by the others chosen and how they are arranged. For more on this, refer to the information in part two, "Instructions for Using the Ocean Oracle."

Behavior Group

1. Angel Wing (Atlantic)
Cyrtopleura costata
MEANING: Determination
EXPLANATION: Despite their fragile appearance, Angel Wings are piddock clams that are capable of boring holes through rock. Through persistence, these excavations take on the Angel Wing's own dimensions, and the customized tomb provides protection.

2. Angel Wing (Pacific)
Barnea digitata
MEANING: Feeling trapped; options seeming unclear
EXPLANATION: As with the Atlantic Angel Wing, this clam bores through rock to create a home. Due to the time and effort involved in excavating their rocky sanctuaries, the holes are very snug fits, and this greatly restricts freedom of movement.

3. Coral
MEANING: Competition
EXPLANATION: Calcium crystals are the essential building blocks for both shells and coral. Live coral compete with mollusks for the dissolved calcium in their immediate surroundings. Scientists believe that

to aid in this competition, coral release a substance that is repugnant to mollusks. Although many species of mollusks find shelter in coral graveyards, few coexist with living coral colonies. (See no. 49, Rapa Snail, for an exception.)

4. Giant Bittersweet
Glycymeris gigantea
MEANING: Concerned with efficiency and accomplishment; disliking waste
EXPLANATION: Almost all mollusks have copper-based blue blood. Bittersweets are one of the rare exceptions that have red blood, due to their iron-based hemoglobin. Iron is a much more efficient oxygen carrier, and it is quite the advantage in oxygen-poor environments where the Bittersweets dwell.

5. Pallid Carrier
Xenophora pallidula
MEANING: Finding that what used to come easily now requires hard work
EXPLANATION: Carrier mollusks collect whatever small shells and other debris surrounds them on the ocean bottom and cement these bits of camouflage to the surface of their shell. Scientists believe that this increase in surface area may prevent the mollusks from sinking in the mud. Since these additions may hamper their mobility, they orient their collection to provide the least amount of drag. This explains why each shell applied to the carrier in this photograph has been fastened with its aperture pointing upward.

6. Sunburst Carrier
Stellaria solaris
MEANING: Preferring to be alone; avoiding attachments
EXPLANATION: Unlike all other species of carrier shells (see no. 5), the Sunburst Carrier forms no attachments at any stage of its life cycle. Attraction to this shell may indicate a belief that equates relationship to pain—from abandonment, loss of identity, or some sort of self-sacrifice. This may be true even if the person seems to be pursuing a relationship. If past experiences have failed to be supportive, subconscious desires to avoid entanglements may result. This person may not realize that he or she is motivated to push others away. Such people already in a relationship may be unconsciously looking for a way out, preferring to be alone. Selecting this carrier shell calls for an examination of beliefs regarding relationships. By recognizing the source of these beliefs, one gains the opportunity to decide whether to maintain or change them. If one chooses to shift perspective, no longer equating relationships with pain and sacrifice, then one can attract a supportive relationship or maintain a stronger connection with the current partner.

7. West Indian Chiton
Chiton tuberculatus
MEANING: Physical or verbal abuse by others
EXPLANATION: Chiton shells are composed of eight separate overlapping plates. This arrangement allows the animals to conform to the contours of the rocks to which they suction themselves. They have enough flexibility to curl up into a ball when molested. When people curl up into a ball, it is often a defensive posture of last resort to ward off an attacker's blows.

8. Vanhyning's Cockle
Dinocardium robustum
MEANING: Great happiness
EXPLANATION: Cockles are noted for having very powerful foot muscles—so strong that they enable these animals to jump. The jumping of this cockle symbolizes exuberance, such as when people are so happy they "jump for joy."

9. Giant Pacific Cockle
Laevicardium elatum
MEANING: Demanding obedience
EXPLANATION: The way this cockle jumps is reminiscent of interactions with a person who expects others to jump through hoops and briskly follow orders. *Note:* Liking this shell may indicate that one is the most demanding of oneself, including the self-imposed need to satisfy the demands of others.

10. Crown Conch
Melongena corona
MEANING: Lawyers, court, legal mediation (and to a lesser degree, problems with authority)
EXPLANATION: Crown Conchs "always get their man." They can attack an animal three times their size and win. They have been observed creeping around their prey and attacking from behind. Sometimes, in a group effort, they will circle their prey and—at the opportune moment, in response to some signal—strike together. This approach is reminiscent of a posse surrounding a villain and recommending surrender. The shell's name comes from its upper region, which resembles a crown head ornament worn by the ruler of a monarchy. The crown symbolizes the government of a country—the ultimate law.

11. Florida Fighting Conch
Strombus alatus
MEANING: Standing one's ground; self-defense
EXPLANATION: Fighting conchs are not aggressive but will strike out to protect themselves if threatened.

12. Lister's Conch
Strombus listeri
MEANING: Going with the flow
EXPLANATION: These conchs are among the few animals that can survive the terrible monsoons near Thailand. While many other forms of sea life perish, the conchs are able to ride out these violent seasonal storms.

13. Scorpion Conch
Lambis scorpius scorpius
MEANING: Maturity; acting older than one's years; responsibility
EXPLANATION: The protrusions from the shell's lip, called digits, do not form until the animal has reached full maturity. Until then, the lip's edge is perfectly smooth. *Note:* Attraction to this shell indicates that a person may have grown up fast, shouldering responsibility at an early age. Conversely, disliking this shell may indicate a reluctance to grow up or some other issue with responsibility.

14. Terebellum Conch
Terebellum terebellum
MEANING: Vigilance; keeping an eye out for danger
EXPLANATION: This conch lives buried underground, but an anatomical adaptation allows it to perceive danger on the surface: its eye is at the tip of a

long stalk encased in a firm tube. Thus protected, the eye is able to penetrate the sandy surface above. This periscope arrangement enables the Terebellum Conch to literally keep an eye out for danger as it rapidly travels beneath the ocean floor.

15. Cone with barnacles
MEANING: Loss of identity; needing to assert oneself
EXPLANATION: Though there are many species of barnacles, they share the common characteristic of attaching themselves to objects underwater. When a barnacle attaches itself to a shell, as its colony multiplies, it covers an increasing amount of the shell's surface area. Eventually, the shell disappears from sight. In a similar pattern, people may give others so much control over their lives that they become swallowed up and lose their identities in the process.

16. Eyed Cowrie
Cypraea argus
MEANING: Desire to make improvements
EXPLANATION: Most univalves accommodate an increase in body size by adding a larger whorl to the bottom of their spiraling shell. Since the animal resides in this largest section of its shell, it is unable to reach the upper portion. The uppermost area, deprived of attention, eventually ages and fades. Cowries, however, approach the problem of increased body size quite differently. They secrete acid to dissolve the interior of their shell while they add new material to the entire external surface. In contrast to the faded older top sections of most univalve shells, the cowrie continually improves its appearance, redecorating its entire shell with newer, brighter colors.

17. Imperial Delphinula
Angaria delphinulus form melanacantha
MEANING: Going at a slower pace in order to flourish; retreating in order to grow
EXPLANATION: In order for the shell's spines to fully develop in length, the Imperial Delphinula must reside in slow, calm, and quiet waters. *Note:* Since quiet time is required to confront a troubling issue, if this shell repulses someone, it indicates that this person may look for distractions to avoid facing or dealing with a problem.

18. Graceful Fig
Ficus gracilis
MEANING: Openness and honesty, as in the expression "What you see is what you get"
EXPLANATION: Fig shells are univalves with a large opening, but they lack an operculum, the door that seals other univalves into their shells. (See no. 43, Cat's Eye operculum.) When a person chooses not to hide behind walls, he or she lives honestly, exposed to all.

19. Flamingo Tongue
Cyphoma gibbosum
MEANING: Possessiveness; territorial behavior
EXPLANATION: Flamingo Tongue males live on sea fans with a harem of females. They will fight off any other encroaching males with the ferocity of a tiger.

20. Ventral Harp
Harpa ventricosa
MEANING: The intended victim will be the victor; a complete reversal; present sacrifice for future reward
EXPLANATION: The harp mollusk has the ability to detach a portion of its foot, which it can later regenerate. This is useful when attacked by a predator such as a crab. While the crab is occupied with this morsel from the harp's foot, the harp secretes mucus, mixes it with sand, and covers the crab. This immobilizes the crab, but rather than escaping, the harp turns the tables and eats the now-vulnerable crab. Just as the harp mollusk sacrifices a portion of its foot, one may be required to make a sacrifice in order to obtain a future reward.

21. Reticulated Cowrie Helmet
Cypraecassis testiculus
MEANING: Confidence; nerve; courage
EXPLANATION: The Latin scientific name for this shell is *testiculus*, based on its resemblance to that part of the male anatomy. Interestingly, while the meaning was originally derived from our culture's association of this particular part of the male anatomy with the quality of courage and self-confidence, years later I came across a photograph of a Reticulated Cowrie Helmet denuding a sea urchin of its spines before consuming it. The accompanying article explained that helmet conchs—which includes cowrie helmets—are the only mollusks that eat sea urchins. They willingly climb over the urchin's sharp spines. These spines pose an intimidating defense for other mollusks, who keep a healthy distance away. Thus, a meaning originally derived from the name and appearance of the shell was corroborated by the behavior of the animal.

22. King Helmet
Cassis tuberosa

MEANING: An ally; a champion (on your behalf)

EXPLANATION: This shell symbolizes a person who is willing to fight for you, a meaning supported by its helmet-like appearance, which is also the source of its name. I once discovered an account written by an alert malacologist (a scientist who studies mollusks) who had managed to photograph two helmet conchs rescuing a third helmet conch in danger. These "lowly invertebrates" recognized that their comrade was in peril and developed a cooperative plan of rescue. *Note:* A person who dislikes this shell may feel let down by someone, causing this person to have difficulty trusting others. This distrust may hinder willingness to delegate responsibility due to the difficulty of relying on anyone else. Also, having experienced the pain of being let down, this person will make an extra effort to fulfill obligations to avoid inflicting that same pain on others.

23. Janthina Snail
Janthina janthina

MEANING: Living in a fantasy world; clinging to the clouds with no desire to be shown anything different; a state of denial

EXPLANATION: Although it is unable to swim, the Janthina lives on the surface of the ocean far from shore. It accomplishes this by attaching itself to a homemade raft of mucus-cemented air bubbles. Its survival depends on clinging to these air bubbles, which is equivalent to the desire to live in a fantasy, for if it becomes dislodged from the raft it will drown. In addition, the animal is blind, indicating a preference to not see the reality.

24. Jingle Shells
Anomia simplex
MEANING: Having a focus that's too one-sided; need for balance (with time, money, energy)
EXPLANATION: As bivalves, Jingle Shells have two valves comprising the shell. You may notice that you rarely, if ever, find both sides of this shell. Through a hole in the lower right valve, the animal sends an anchor—called a byssus plug, constructed from filamentous threads it produces—to secure itself to a stable foundation. When the animal dies, the shells separate so that the upper left valve washes up on beaches. It is much rarer to encounter the more fragile right side.

25. Thorned Latirus
Opeatostoma pseudodon
MEANING: Leverage; positional advantage; power to act effectively
EXPLANATION: The Latirus uses the thorny structure extending from the base of its shell as leverage to pry open its prey.

26. Giant Lima Clam
Acesta phillipinensis
MEANING: Desiring privacy over personal matters; discomfort over exposure of personal information
EXPLANATION: Lima, or file clams, are poor swimmers and can't rely on this skill to evade predatory fish. However, once caught, their sticky, detachable tentacles immediately break off in a pursuer's mouth. The tentacles wrap around each other, effectively gluing the fish's mouth shut. With this borrowed time, the clams employ one more marvelous adaptation:

They are capable of producing more byssus threads (filamentous strings) than any other mollusk—enough to form nests. These sanctuaries provide a place into which they can burrow to make their escape. The meaning of this shell is derived from this combination of stopping someone from talking and taking refuge in one's private quarters.

27. Plate Limpet
Acmaea testudinalis
MEANING: Tenacious; stubborn
EXPLANATION: By applying suction, the limpet remains attached to intertidal rocks, unaffected by pounding waves. Varying accounts claim it takes anywhere from thirty to seventy pounds of pressure per square inch to pry a limpet off a rock against its will.

28. Long-Ribbed Limpet
Patella longicosta
MEANING: Looking for where the grass is greener but needing to look in one's own backyard; looking for answers outside oneself when they reside within
EXPLANATION: Limpets live on rocks by suctioning to hollow depressions, called scars, which they create with acid secretions. They leave these depressions at night searching for food. No matter where their travels take them, they return to the identical scar from which they came. Even when scientists reorient the rock, the limpets find their original "homes." With this *Wizard of Oz*–like sentiment that "there is no place like home," this shell indicates that instead of looking for outside sources of advice, you should look inside yourself.

29. Patella Limpet
Patella miniata
MEANING: Caretaker
EXPLANATION: The Patella Limpet tends a garden of Ralfsia algae, its only food source. The limpet defends its garden by removing other algae species and by pushing away or partially paralyzing invading animals. Without the limpet's devoted care, the Ralfsia would disappear from overgrazing by other animals or competition from other algae.

30. Delessert's Lyria
Lyria delessertiana
MEANING: Pursuit of a relationship causing problems and compromising other situations
EXPLANATION: Lyria reside in deep water. They will, however, venture into shallow water to mate. This is the only time capture is possible. It is the mating instinct—and hormones—that causes a problem for Lyria. In human terms, this translates to body chemistry creating compromising situations for oneself or others.

31. Shark's Eye Moon Snail
Neverita duplicata
MEANING: Blowing things out of proportion
EXPLANATION: Moon snails can absorb water into their bodies, inflating themselves to three or four times the size of their shells. Some species of moon snails can completely envelope their shells, burying them in the midst of their soft bodies. *Note:* Blowing things out of proportion, or making mountains out of molehills, occurs because someone equates attention with love. While many "moon snail" people will surround themselves with various disasters—even physical illness—

in order to garner attention, the moon snail makes no judgment over what experience gets inflated. Therefore, if one so chooses, attention can be obtained by increasing the wonderful experiences in life.

32. Pink Mouth Murex
Phyllonotus erythrostomus

MEANING: Issues that stem from childhood; subconscious childhood beliefs impacting life choices

EXPLANATION: The females of this species travel into deep water to lay eggs in communal masses. Each female is capable of producing many egg capsules. It is not unusual for a female to become trapped among the cumulative millions of eggs in this mass and die. This represents the stranglehold that beliefs formulated in childhood can have on our lives. Survival behaviors we developed as children may no longer serve us as adults. Persons selecting this shell may benefit from inner-child work.

33. Blue Mussel
Mytilus edulis

MEANING: Indebtedness; having strings attached

EXPLANATION: Mussels secrete a liquid material that quickly hardens into stringy filamentous threads called byssus. These threads serve as anchors to wharves and rocks and thus prevent the mussels from becoming dislodged and damaged by the tides. When a mussel does relocate, it begins the journey by loosening a few threads and repositioning them. Once these are secure, it moves a few more threads to the new position. This process continues until the animal is fully relocated. By this means, mussels are capable of climbing up wooden piers or to more desirable rocky locales. Attaching to these stable foundations, they are able to survive the pounding waves. Since, literally, there are strings attached to the mussel's every move, the person who chooses this shell may hold a "strings attached" view of human nature. This belief doesn't mean that these people are not generous, however. But their unrecognized, hidden motivation for generosity comes from the belief that the other person will be indebted should they ever need assistance. Conversely, generous acts arouse suspicion in these people, as they don't trust that others could be motivated out of pure altruism, and they wonder what they will owe in exchange.

34. Freshwater Mussel
Unio complanatus
MEANING: Parasite; mooch; exposure to someone looking for a free ride
EXPLANATION: In freshwater, the life cycles of mussels include a parasitic larval stage, called glochidium, during which they possess hook-like structures for attaching to host fish. They absorb nutrients from their host's blood while undergoing metamorphosis to a more mature phase of their life cycle. Once this is achieved, they drop off the fish and form a shell. A parasitic person choosing this mussel is content to camp out in your home, never offering assistance and eating you out of house and home. This is distinct from the vampire (no. 60, Maculated Dwarf Triton) who drains your energy just by being in your presence.

35. Nassa Snail
Nassarius vibex
MEANING: Machiavellian; walking over people to get what one wants; believing that the ends justify the means
EXPLANATION: Nassa snails are scavengers that travel in large armies along the ocean bottom. Their numbers are so vast that they crawl over each other to find room to walk. *Note:* This shell may refer to the person who chooses it or to someone of his or her acquaintance.

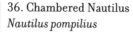

36. Chambered Nautilus
Nautilus pompilius
MEANING: Something from the past returning as part of a pattern; mistakenly thinking the door is closed on a past event

EXPLANATION: The bisected shell of a Chambered Nautilus exposes the inner chambers for which it is aptly named. As the young mollusk's body grows and its shell becomes too confining, it walls off the section previously occupied and builds a larger addition or "chamber" onto its shell. A connecting channel that pierces through all previous chambers remains. The mollusk uses this channel to control its buoyancy in the ocean. (See no. 38, Pearly Nautilus.) Although the earlier chambers appear to be sealed off, the channel provides the means to connect with them. *Note:* Selecting this shell indicates an emotional life experience someone hopes to forget, something that is not an isolated experience but part of a pattern. Even if the people involved change, the same experience will likely be repeated with someone else. Furthermore, the circumstances will intensify each time until a pinnacle is reached that can't be ignored. Taking the opportunity to confront this situation can heal not only the current event but also all those that preceded it. With healing comes a new perspective, and the pattern need no longer be repeated.

37. Paper Nautilus
Argonauta argo
MEANING: Spiritual birth; great awakening
EXPLANATION: The Paper Nautilus, or Argonaut, like its cousin the octopus, has eight arms. Unlike other nautilus species, the Argonaut does not possess a shell. The shell pictured is a by-product of the female Argonaut. Two of her eight arms end in enlarged paddles. When she produces

eggs, these paddles secrete the parchment-like material for this "shell," which serves as a buoyant cradle for mother and eggs. Since this shell represents a birthplace, it symbolizes spiritual birth, or a great awakening.

38. Pearly Nautilus
Nautilus pompilius
MEANING: Pressure; stress
EXPLANATION: As mentioned with the Chambered Nautilus (see no. 36), the nautilus shell is constructed with a series of incrementally larger compartments, or chambers. The newest and largest is attached as the animal outgrows its current residence. The nautilus floods its empty back chambers with water to increase its depth in the ocean. When it wants to rise, it forces gas through a tube, called a siphuncle, which runs back through the connecting channel piercing the center of each chamber. The pressurized gas expels the fluid contents and allows the animal to ascend. Thus, the nautilus employs pressurized gas as a means to control its buoyancy. The back chambers serve as ballast tanks, which is the same principle utilized by the submarine, one model of which was aptly named the *Nautilus*.

39. Mercado's Nutmeg
Scalptia mercadoi
MEANING: Futility; beating your head against a wall; being impenetrable
EXPLANATION: The Mercado's Nutmeg deposits calcium shell material in thickened ribs. This provides additional protection from penetration by predators.

40. Miller's Nutmeg
Trigonostoma milleri

MEANING: Living in the now; detachment from negative past experiences and future expectations

EXPLANATION: Other than worm shells, it is rare to find a univalve mollusk whose shell whorls are not sutured together. The disconnected whorls of worm shells are due to uncontrolled growth, evidenced by their haphazard direction (see no. 65, West Indian Worm Shell). In marked contrast to this approach to shell growth, the Miller's Nutmeg produces a shell in deliberate, neatly stacked, unattached coils.

41. Lettered Olive
Oliva sayana

MEANING: Invitation to opportunity

EXPLANATION: The olive mollusk is incredibly sensitive to the chemical composition of its environment. The animal's chemoreceptors analyze the waste materials of its prey as they are carried along by the ocean, a capability that allows it to detect dead animals only minutes after their death. By capitalizing on this information, the olive can get a meal before the competition even knows there is one to be had.

42. Onion Shell
Melapium elatum

MEANING: Devotion and dedication, especially regarding motherhood

EXPLANATION: Whatever form mollusk reproduction takes, it generally involves the production of hundreds, if not thousands, of eggs. The parents then abandon these eggs to fate. In a rare departure from this format, the female onion mollusk produces only a couple of eggs and attaches them directly to her shell. This devotion greatly enhances their chances for survival.

43. Cat's Eye operculum

MEANING: Desire to protect and insulate oneself

EXPLANATION: The Cat's Eye is the operculum found on the Tapestry Turban mollusk. The operculum is not a shell; it is a hardened portion of the univalve mollusk. Located on the bottom of its foot, the operculum is the last portion of the mollusk to be pulled into its shell. It functions as a trap door, sealing off the opening and protecting the vulnerable mollusk inside.

44. Black-Lipped Pearl Oyster
Pinctada margaritifera

MEANING: Looking for the gift connected to the situation; beauty from irritation

EXPLANATION: A pearl is created by an oyster's effort to dull the irritation caused by a grain of sand or another substance that has found its way into the shell. By wrapping the grain in many layers of nacre (the pearly substance the oyster secretes to form the inner lining of its shell), a smooth, pearly object is formed. Taking advantage of the oyster's ability to secrete nacre, humans have produced cultured pearls. Proceeding delicately, man has been able to introduce irritants of many shapes to be wrapped by the pearly material.

45. Pelican's Foot
Aporrhais pespelecani

MEANING: Feeling awkward; being clumsy

EXPLANATION: This mollusk's movements are slow and awkward.

46. Stiff Pen
Atrina rigida

MEANING: Altruism; concern for the welfare of others; selflessness

EXPLANATION: Scientists have observed small shrimp and crabs living inside the shells of the Stiff Pen for shelter and protection. Thus far, they have found no mutual benefit for the pen mollusk from this arrangement. Attraction to this shell indicates the desire to give to those less fortunate, with no expectation of receiving anything in return. *Note:* Most people disliking this shell are fully prepared to receive no financial reward for their gifts. Although their intent is laudable, however, it bears mentioning that in addition to receiving no money, it is possible that one may receive neither respect nor love in return as well. The challenge with this shell is to be aware of what asking for nothing in return entails. The reality of receiving no reward for service may be more difficult than anticipated.

47. Pheasant Shell
Phasianella australis

MEANING: Hesitant to commit; feeling one's way; playing it safe

EXPLANATION: The pheasant mollusk extends several filamentous foot feelers, cautiously testing the waters before it journeys forth.

48. Coronate Prickly-winkle
Tectarius coronatus

MEANING: Extremely tolerant of harsh conditions; avoiding confrontation; not standing up for oneself

EXPLANATION: Some species of winkles live in very harsh environments. They endure extreme heat, high salinity, dehydration, or drowning rains. Tolerating these horrible conditions may be preferable to competing for food with other species living in more favorable environments.

49. Rapa Snail
Rapa rapa
MEANING: Putting the competition at ease; being well-liked
EXPLANATION: To build their shells, mollusks compete with coral for the calcium in the water. (See no. 3.) As protection, it is surmised that living coral release a substance that mollusks find repugnant. It is therefore unusual to find mollusks coexisting with live coral. One exception, the Rapa Snail, lives in colonies deep within spongy Pacific reef coral.

50. Zigzag Scallop
Pecten ziczac
MEANING: Engaging in behaviors that don't produce the desired outcome; confusion; the need for a change in direction to find clarity
EXPLANATION: Scallops clap their shells together to great effect. This allows them to swim rapidly by jet propulsion. Some swim in a zigzag pattern, changing course to take any direction they desire. They may also clap their shells together as they dive into mud. This creates a murky environment, making them more difficult to spot by enemies and aiding them in eluding capture. This deliberate muddying of the waters represents extraneous information that detracts from the clarity of a situation and increases confusion.

51. Lion's Paw Scallop

Lyropecten nodosa

MEANING: Discovering that a person thought to be an enemy turns out to be a friend or someone who provides a service for growth

EXPLANATION: The shell of the Lion's Paw Scallop has enlarged hollow areas, called "knuckles," that the animal fills with fluid to provide extra defense. These knuckles resemble the knuckles that protrude when a human hand is closed into a fist. As is sometimes the case with people, the scallop's knuckles are for the purpose of protection. The person who picks this shell may perceive someone as an enemy without realizing that he or she may actually have the person's best interests at heart. It is also possible that even without good intentions his or her actions will force the person to grow in ways never dreamed possible. Had life not become uncomfortable, or had support not been withheld, skills and abilities that will greatly enhance growth might never have been discovered. *Note:* This shell may require some soul-searching. It may help the healing process if it is possible to recognize the gift derived from the experience; perhaps that will ease the pain endured along the way.

52. Sea Horse

MEANING: Being the ideal husband or father, or any nurturing male

EXPLANATION: Although not a mollusk, the sea horse cohabits with mollusks, and the male's unique behavior adds to the shell vocabulary. For its role in the birth process, the male sea horse is remarkable in the animal kingdom. Though the female lays the eggs, the male is equipped with a pouch into which the eggs are transferred. There, they are nurtured and remain until contractions release the infant sea horses into the ocean.

53. Atlantic Slipper
Crepidula fornacata
MEANING: Challenging stereotypes; pushing limits
EXPLANATION: Slipper shells live atop one another in colonies. The smallest shells on top are young males, and the older, larger shells at the base are females. The females release a steady supply of hormone. When a female dies, the hormone level is altered, resulting in the transformation of the oldest, lowest male slipper shell into a female. This new female subsequently gives birth to the next generation of males, which take their positions at the top of the colony. Thus, each slipper shell experiences life as both genders, beginning its life cycle as a male and completing it as a female. This shell encourages men to allow their feminine side to flourish and women to express their male energy. Beyond this, it encourages any form of pushing the envelope and defying the limiting ideas or labels prevailing at the time. Selecting this shell indicates a desire to break through barriers in the interest of establishing equality.

54. Green Tree Snail
Papuina pulcherrima
MEANING: Willingness to change one's comfort zone
EXPLANATION: During the dry winter season, these New Guinea land snails enter a period of inactivity called aestivation. They seal up their shells with mucus plugs, preventing water loss while allowing oxygen to pass. They hibernate in this fashion until comfortable living conditions are restored to their environment. Only then do they regain an active lifestyle as they venture out of hiding. *Note:* This shell is an excellent barometer of a person's comfort zone in relation to a particular issue. Attraction to this shell indicates readiness to change; repulsion indicates the person isn't ready to change.

55. Placostylus Land Snail
Placostylus
MEANING: Getting what you wish for; nothing standing in the way
EXPLANATION: Land snails secrete mucus to facilitate their gliding mobility. They have been observed crawling over an upended razor blade, completely unharmed by the sharp edge. *Note:* A person attracted to this shell may be experiencing the same ease as desires are fulfilled. Before wishing for something, however, it's important to carefully consider all the ramifications if the dream becomes reality—and the path by which it does so.

56. Candy-Stripe Tree Snail
Liguus virgineus
MEANING: Home, property, material possessions
EXPLANATION: Because these Haitian snails are so admired for their beauty, efforts were made to import them to Florida. This experiment failed dismally, and scientists discovered that a particular Haitian tree is the only home that will sustain these animals.

57. Wavy-Edge Spindle
Fusinus undatus
MEANING: Partner, helper
EXPLANATION: Spindle shells live in pairs on the sandy bottom of the ocean.

58. Starfish
MEANING: Surviving something disgusting and stomach-turning
EXPLANATION: The meanings here are derived from two unusual starfish characteristics: Firstly, when cut into sections, each piece of a starfish is capable of regenerating into a completely new starfish. Since starfish dine on oysters, they are the bane of oyster fishermen's existence. Some innovative fishermen, in an effort to reduce the starfish population in their area, hauled as many starfish as they could aboard their fishing boats and chopped them into pieces. They then tossed these sections of starfish back into the sea, unknowingly multiplying their problem. Secondly, once a starfish has captured and pried open an oyster, it turns its own stomach out of its mouth and into the oyster's valves. After absorbing the nutrients provided by this meal, the starfish swallows its stomach back into its body.

59. Shinbone Tibia
Tibia fusus fusus
MEANING: Feeling left out or being kept in the dark; things going over one's head
EXPLANATION: This intricately sculpted shell never sees the light of day. The mollusk lives buried upside down beneath the ground with just the tip of the bottom of its shell breaking the surface. Although the animal has eyes, its head is positioned too deep in the ground for the sun's rays to penetrate. Engulfed in darkness, its vision is greatly impaired.

60. Maculated Dwarf Triton
Colubraria muricata

MEANING: Being drained; interacting with an exhausting person (a human vampire)

EXPLANATION: Some species of Dwarf Tritons exhibit vampire-like behavior. Photographs have captured one triton penetrating through the mucus barrier of a sleeping parrotfish and another probing a shark's scar tissue. Both animals are intent on sucking the hosts' blood to obtain nutrients. In human terms, vampire behavior occurs when someone drains another of energy.

61. Atlantic Trumpet Triton
Charonia variegata

MEANING: Being numb to feelings and in denial of emotions

EXPLANATION: Tritons emit a chemical to anesthetize their prey. With the prey effectively numbed and immobilized, it loses any potential to mount a defense.

62. Banded Tulip
Fasciolaria lilium hunteria

MEANING: Not stopping to smell the roses; not appreciating life

EXPLANATION: Mollusks have a diverse range of feeding habits. Some are strict vegetarians, others are carnivores. A few, such as this tulip, are cannibals. Stopping to smell the roses indicates an appreciation for all life. By killing their own kind, these mollusks reveal a lack of value for any life.

63. Common Tusk
Dentalium vulgare
MEANING: Perceiving someone as heartless
EXPLANATION: At one time, tusk mollusks were
thought to have no heart. Scientists believed that
blood circulation was accomplished by contractions
of the foot muscle. It is now known that they do possess a very
undeveloped, rudimentary heart.

64. Whelk egg case
MEANING: Pregnancy, birth, babies
EXPLANATION: This is a case formed by the female
whelk to surround and protect her eggs before
they hatch.

65. West Indian Worm Shell
Vermicularia spirata
MEANING: Something completely out of one's control; something spoiled
EXPLANATION: Worm shells are not related to
worms at all; they are the creation of mollusks whose
shells undergo uncontrolled coiling. Instead of the neat symmetri-
cal spirals most univalves produce, worm shells have no pattern to
their coils.

Interaction Group

66. Paua Abalone
Haliotis iris
MEANING: Seeing past the exterior, as in the expression "Don't judge a book by its cover"
EXPLANATION: In its natural state, the abalone is covered with barnacles and tube worms and does not draw attention. If we scrape off this outer surface, an iridescent paua material, sometimes termed "sea opal," lies just beneath. Greatly valued for its beauty, this paua is often used by jewelers to fashion colorful bracelets, earrings, and pins.

67. Red Abalone
Haliotis rufescens
MEANING: Needing to heal emotionally to avoid physical problems
EXPLANATION: The abalone shell is often used as a vessel to contain sage during modern smudging ceremonies. (The smoke from the burning sage purifies the environmental energy.) In addition, extracts from the abalone animal have been used medicinally against penicillin-resistant strains of staph, strep, and typhus. As these functions indicate, the abalone can address issues at the energetic/emotional stage, which may preempt them from occurring at the physical level.

68. Japanese Babylon
Babylonia japonica
MEANING: Getting in touch with one's inner child; playing more, free from adult constraints
EXPLANATION: In Japan, children use these shells as spinning-top toys.

69. Zoned Paper Bubble
Hydatina zonata
MEANING: Secret, closeted behavior
EXPLANATION: Some bubble mollusks are barely
able to fit within the confines of their shells. To maxi-
mize the available protective space, as they lack

operculums (see no. 43, Cat's Eye), they empty the contents of their
stomachs before retracting into their shells. This characteristic,
and the fact that bubble mollusks only eat when buried underground, foiled scientists' efforts to discover their eating habits for
many years. Their purging behavior resembles bulimia, a condition in which people empty the contents of their stomachs after
consuming a meal. Although the human purpose is generally for
weight control, the behavior is conducted in secret, and it is just
one of many possible closeted human behaviors. Bubble mollusks
are also hermaphrodites; they contain the sex organs of both
genders and perform both roles for each other. Although common
in the molluscan world, such sexual variety in the human world
often necessitates secrecy.

70. Buccinum Whelk
Buccinum undatum
MEANING: Needing to "come clean" or confess
something
EXPLANATION: Years ago, when soap was prohibi-
tively expensive, sailors used the round egg cases of

the Buccinum Whelk as scrub balls in lieu of soap. *Note:* It is possible that this shell may represent something repressed or denied
from awareness until now.

71. Indian Chank
Turbinella pyrum
MEANING: Something or someone held sacred or dear
EXPLANATION: In India, a particular form of this chank shell is placed on religious altars as a symbol of adoration. This practice stems from the Hindu belief that the devil once hid the Hindu sacred writings in the ocean, and their god, Vishnu, found them in a left-handed chank shell. (See no. 79, Marble Cone, for an explanation of "left-handedness.") The rare, left-handed versions of these shells are displayed on altars. The more common, right-handed versions are cut into bangle bracelets. Statues of Vishnu depict him holding the sacred chank shell. (See no. 105, Lightning Whelk, for more about left-handedness.)

72. Quahog Clam
Mercenaria mercenaria
MEANING: Heart health, blood pressure, doctors, and hospitals
EXPLANATION: Within the same species of mollusk, one organ may be quite advanced in development while another organ is poorly developed or completely lacking. This is the case with the clam. Although the clam lacks a head, it does have the most complex heart of the entire molluscan kingdom. The clam's heart is composed of three chambers with a pacemaker that establishes the beat. This resemblance to our own four-chambered heart and pacemaker is not lost on scientists. In an effort to gain valuable insight into the workings of our hearts, they have performed many studies testing the effects of curare, nicotine, and other chemicals on nerve impulses to the clam's heart. In addition, scientists have found an extract from these hard-shelled clams, called mercinine, that is an effective growth inhibitor of cancers in laboratory mice.

73. Heart Cockle
Corculum cardissa
MEANING: Love, romance
EXPLANATION: The natural heart shape formed by the two halves of this bivalve led sailors to present these shells to their sweethearts as "sailor's valentines."

74. Pink Conch
Strombus gigas
MEANING: Listening to one's heart
EXPLANATION: People enjoy holding this shell to their ear, convinced they are listening to the sound of the ocean. Actually, the shell amplifies the sound of blood circulating within the ear. Since the human heart pumps this blood, we are, in effect, listening to our own hearts. Occasionally, this animal produces pink pearls, which can be considered as gems of wisdom coming from the heart.

75. Arthritic Spider Conch
Lambis chiragra
MEANING: Changing residence, or major change within a residence; someone moving in or out
EXPLANATION: There is a mystery regarding spider conchs and the Aztec Indians who resided in Mexico centuries ago. The Aztec god Quetzalcoatl is often depicted wearing a spider conch. However, these shells are found in the South Pacific, thousands of miles from Mexico. When one considers that the Aztecs lacked the transportation to enable them to travel this far, how did they know of the existence of this shell? Speculation exists that a species of this conch at one time existed near Mexico and either left the area or became extinct.

76. Geography Cone
Conus geographus
MEANING: Putting past negative behavior to positive use
EXPLANATION: All cone mollusks possess a poison gland in their head that is attached by a tube to harpoon-like teeth. The teeth deliver a poisonous injection that, depending on the cone species, can have a range of effects on man. The Geography and Textile Cones (see no. 80) contain the most toxic poisons. These carnivores' injections function as a neurotoxin, similar to snake venom, that paralyzes their prey. Together, these two species are accountable for at least ten cases of fatalities to man. However, with slight alterations, the paralyzing toxins of the Geography Cone have been employed successfully by doctors to combat human tremors. Attraction to this shell indicates a positive, beneficial use for a destructive, negative behavior. For example, a reformed criminal, with his unique insights, might instruct others on crime prevention. The person selecting this shell may find a useful purpose for any negativity in his or her life.

77. Glory of India Cone
Conus milneedwardsi
MEANING: Reaping rewards for past good deeds
EXPLANATION: In 1740, the first recorded specimen of this shell was found, and it was unknown where more might be located. In the 1890s, three more specimens were found near India when an underwater telegraph cable was raised for cleaning. The cleaning process revealed these cones hidden underneath a heavy encrustation of plant and animal life. Man's considerable efforts to raise and clean this cable were rewarded with this unexpected treasure. These rare shells were once worth a fortune; even today they are still not inexpensive, and they have always been prized for their beauty.

78. Hirase Cone
Conus hirasei
MEANING: Being a perfectionist; being highly critical; one's inner judge
EXPLANATION: Divers who gather these shells to sell have been known to paint stripes on some specimens to correct "errors." This compulsion to improve on nature captures the essence of those attracted to this shell. Never satisfied, a person may place the highest expectations on him or herself.

79. Marble Cone
Conus marmoreus
MEANING: Ruin; disappointment
EXPLANATION: In 1650, the Dutch artist Rembrandt was commissioned to make an etching of the Marble Cone for an illustrated book of seashells. After carefully etching his drawing on a metal plate with acid, he neglected to consider that a print made from an etching will appear as its mirror image. With most subjects this may not matter, but with seashells it is crucial. If you hold a univalve shell so that the top, or apex, is pointing up and the opening, or aperture, is facing you (as in this photo), you will discover that almost every univalve spirals in a clockwise direction and opens on the right, or dextral, side. These shells are naturally right-handed. Only through a rare mutation will you find left-handed versions of some of these shells opening on the left, or sinistral, side (see no. 105, Lightning Whelk, for one such exception). The print resulting from Rembrandt's etching depicted a normally right-handed shell as if it were left-handed. Since this diametrically opposed the shell's appearance, the etching could not appear in the book for which it was intended.

80. Textile Cone
Conus textile
MEANING: Death; transformation; eliminating bag-
gage no longer needed
EXPLANATION: Textile Cones are sometimes used by
shell collectors to clean cowrie shells. The entry to a
cowrie shell is a very narrow slit (see no. 85, Tiger Cowrie). This
makes removal of the mollusk difficult for humans. The poisonous
barb of the Textile Cone is able to kill and digest the mollusk, leaving the cowrie shell in pristine condition (see no. 76, Geography
Cone, for more on cone-shell poisons). Thus, the cone absorbs the
nutrients it needs but leaves the unnecessary shell intact.

Cowries
Most univalves live inside their shells. Accordingly, the interior of
the shells is smooth in order to prevent damage to the mollusks' soft
bodies. Cowries, however, like to wrap themselves around the outside of their shells, requiring a smooth exterior shell surface, which
gives the shell a polished appearance. The underside of these shells
contains the identifying characteristic of all cowries: a central
puckered ridge that ancient Europeans thought resembled the
genital tract of their sows (female pigs). With this inspiration, they
called these shells *porcellana*, which translates as "little pig." When
Marco Polo returned from China with never-before-seen glazed
pottery, the surface so resembled these porcellana shells that the
Europeans called the pottery *porcelain*. Hence, the derivation of the
word porcelain comes from man's interaction with cowrie shells.

Cowries have been used by humans in many ways throughout
history. In ancient Egypt, small cowries were placed in mummy eye
sockets for vision in the afterlife. In Asia, because of the resemblance to female reproductive organs, pregnant women hold
cowries to facilitate childbirth. The most widespread use of cowries
was as currency. Entire trade routes were established around the

supply of a particular species of Money Cowrie. In order to accommodate the many interactions with cowries, I have assigned a variety of meanings to shells 81 through 85 based on specific cowrie uses in various locations throughout the world.

81. Golden Cowrie
Cypraea aurantium
MEANING: Feeling cursed; a run of bad luck
EXPLANATION: These rare shells, found near the Fiji Islands, were worn by chieftains who believed that their souls were encased in the cowrie. To protect this precious cargo, they placed a curse—similar to the Hope Diamond curse—on anyone else who tried to possess a Golden Cowrie. Due to their rarity, these shells were difficult to come by and cost a fortune. Ironically, legend has it that anyone owning one of these shells suffered as a consequence.

82. Idol's Eye Cowrie
Cypraea asellus
MEANING: Seeing things other people don't; intuition
EXPLANATION: As noted in the introduction to this section, Egyptians placed small cowries in mummy eye sockets for vision in the afterlife. In a similar fashion, this cowrie, as its name implies, is used in the eye sockets of Polynesian idols.

83. Isabella Cowrie
Cypraea isabella
MEANING: Uncontrollable fear; panic
EXPLANATION: The explanation for this meaning may be somewhat unflattering to its namesake, Queen Isabella of Spain. It isn't clear whether this is because her subjects did not think her courageous or because they questioned

her hygiene, but the stories agree that they likened the appearance of this shell to the queen's shorts (underwear). When faced with a frightening situation, we may lose control of our bowels and soil our underwear, and that is what her subjects referenced when they saw the streaked pattern on this shell.

84. Money Cowrie
Cypraea moneta
MEANING: Money; abundance; prosperity
EXPLANATION: These shells are quite ubiquitous and have been used as a means of exchange between many countries. African traders used money cowries to purchase Chinese silk. The Chinese traded cowries with Russian trappers for sealskins from Alaska. The Russians used cowries to purchase goods from the West Coast Native Americans who, in turn, traded with tribes all the way to New England. As the number of cowries became too cumbersome to carry, they were sliced into disks, eventually paving the way for replacement with coins.

85. Tiger Cowrie
Cypraea tigris
MEANING: Possessing great faith; having no fear
EXPLANATION: As mentioned in the introduction to this section, the underside of a cowrie shell resembles the female reproductive tract. Perhaps for this reason, cowries became associated with the womb, and the women of Pompeii wore cowries in an effort to prevent sterility. Today, some Asian women ease their fears during childbirth by holding a cowrie shell in each hand. In Japan, these cowries are called *koyasu-gai*, "peaceful child shells." *Note:* This shell does not apply exclusively to physical birth. It may attract those in the "birthing process" of any creative endeavor.

86. Cuttlefish bone
Sepia officinalis
MEANING: Being a writer; being a skilled communicator
EXPLANATION: The cuttlefish is a member of the cephalopod class of mollusks. Along with other members of this class, including the octopus and squid, these animals expel an inky substance to obscure themselves from pursuing enemies. Man has used these cuttlefish, called Sepia squid, as a source of sepia ink for writing instruments. This internal shell, called a pen, resembles antique quills that were used for many years as writing implements. *Note:* A person attracted to this cuttlefish bone may find journaling beneficial.

87. Egg Cowrie
Ovula ovum
MEANING: Hiding emotions behind a mask; false bravado
EXPLANATION: New Guinea warriors attach two egg cowries to either end of a swatch of fabric. Gripping the material between their teeth, the warriors' mouths are flanked by the downward curving apertures of the two cowries. This "mask" effectively triples their menacing expression and is designed to frighten their enemies. False bravado—declaring we are fine when inside we are not fine at all—is one example of the way we mask our emotions.

88. Imperial Harp
Harpa costata
MEANING: Changing negative behaviors, voluntarily or by force
EXPLANATION: This is the national shell of Mauritius. In an effort to prevent the shell's extinction, the country requested that tourists refrain from collecting them. As this

request was consistently ignored, it is now against the law to take one of these shells.

89. Purple Dye Murex (Purpura Murex)
Bolinus brandaris

MEANING: Being treated as special or elite; favoritism

EXPLANATION: The word *purple* comes from the Purpura Murex. In ancient Phoenicia, it was discovered that the Purpura Murex secreted a milky fluid which turned to the color we now call purple when exposed to sunlight. There hadn't been many methods for coloring cloth, and this discovery led to a process for dyeing cloth purple by boiling it to hasten the color shift. Thousands of mollusks were sacrificed to obtain enough dye for one pound of cloth. This made the cloth so prohibitively expensive that only royalty could afford it. In addition, the dye smelled terrible, which required the wearer to mask the odor with perfume—another costly item. Because only royalty could afford this cloth, purple became the traditional regal color.

90. American Thorny Oyster
Spondylus americanus

MEANING: Unconsciously expecting plans to backfire; unwittingly sabotaging oneself

EXPLANATION: During the 1700s, when these shells were very rare, their cost was beyond most people's means. Undeterred, Sir Louis Richard, a serious shell collector, traded his wife's best silver for a specimen. He did this without her knowledge, replacing the silver pieces with tin. With his new shell in his back pocket, he returned home to a very angry wife. Her berating so startled him that he sat down—immediately breaking the shell he had plotted so carefully to obtain.

91. Pacific Thorny Oyster
Spondylus princeps
MEANING: Depending on someone or something for survival
EXPLANATION: Ancient Andean cultures believed that their gods controlled every aspect of their world. Survival depended on seeking the gods' favor. To this end, human sacrifices were offered as "food" to appease the gods. It was hoped that these sacrifices would bring rewards in the form of much-needed rain for their crops. Eventually, the practice of human sacrifices came into disfavor. Because of their resemblance to the color of human blood, these oysters became the new "food for the gods."

92. Common Periwinkle
Littorina littorea
MEANING: A good friend
EXPLANATION: Periwinkles feed on the seaweed that can smother oysters. Sometimes oyster fishermen place buckets of periwinkles in oyster beds. Since this enhances oyster production, periwinkles have been called the oysterman's friend. (See no. 58, Starfish, for an oysterman's enemy.)

93. Wide-Mouthed Purpura
Purpura patula
MEANING: Farsightedness; seeing the big picture; working for the good of all
EXPLANATION: Like no. 89, the Purple Dye Murex, this purpura mollusk also secretes a fluid that yields a purple dye. However, rather than sacrifice them in pursuit of the dye, as was the custom in ancient Phoenicia, Central American natives during the sixteenth and seventeenth centuries learned to "milk" them. This procedure permits the fluid to be obtained from live mollusks and allows the animals to continue producing future

dye material. This technique manages to increase dye production while sparing the animal, so both humans and animals benefit.

94. Razor Clam
Ensis siliqua

MEANING: Compassion, sympathy, mercy

EXPLANATION: The razor clam's streamlined shape enables it to dig five to six feet underground at a pace that exceeds a man with a shovel. Recognizing the futility of trying to dig these clams out of their burrows, people trying to harvest them sprinkle the ground above the clams' holes with coarse salt, which forces the clams to surface in order to rid themselves of the bitter salt. Surfacing places them in peril, but the overriding need to rid their systems of bitterness takes priority. When we put aside all bitterness in an effort to sympathize with another's suffering, we are able to display compassion. The ultimate sign of compassion enables us to treat an enemy with mercy and kindness.

95. Sand Dollar

MEANING: Something being overlooked; the connection between the divine and one's own role in all life experiences, both good and bad

EXPLANATION: Much has been written comparing the appearance of the sand dollar to various aspects of the life of Jesus. There are five slits depicting his wounds—four from the nails, one from a spear. Impressions of an Easter lily and a poinsettia appear on the front and back surface respectively. When a sand dollar is broken, the animal's loose teeth resemble white doves. Whatever your religious beliefs—whether you consider Jesus to be the Son of God or a master teacher—Jesus represents the human connection to divinity. We are all composed of the same divine energy, and if the sand dollar contains evidence of God dwelling within it, it reflects the fact that God dwells within all of us.

We are powerful beings who create, or co-create, our lives based on our belief system. When we experience difficulties, it may be difficult to accept the notion that we create our misery. The good news is that we are not victims. We have the power to create a hell on Earth or a paradise. Through awareness, the choice is ours.

96. St. James Scallop
Pecten maximus jacobaeus
MEANING: Being someone's hero; a hero's journey
EXPLANATION: When ancient visitors made the pilgrimage to the shrine of St. James the Apostle in Compestella, Spain, they adorned their hat brims with scallop shells native to the area. Crusaders used scallop mementos as clothing ornaments on their return journey from the Holy Wars. These sacred journeys were eventually immortalized in British heraldry, and scallops were depicted on British coats of arms as symbols of heroic family ancestors who fought in the crusades or made the pilgrimage to the shrine of Saint James. Another link to heroism occurred when the scallop became the symbol for the Knights of the Garter, an order of British knighthood of which Sir Winston Churchill was a member.

97. Westralis Slit Shell
Pleurotomaria westralis
MEANING: Something elusive or difficult to obtain
EXPLANATION: Slit shells dwell at great depths in the ocean and are not enticed by bait, which makes capture difficult. Due to this elusiveness, these shells were traditionally only rarely seen in collections. During the reign of Japanese Emperor Hirohito, an avid conchologist, one species of slit shell was named the Emperor Slit Shell. No one was allowed to possess this shell except the emperor or someone he had directly bestowed it on as a gift, so owning one meant great prestige.

98. African Land Snail
Achitina zebra
MEANING: Massive devastation; a destructive force affecting many
EXPLANATION: These vegetarian land snails destroy crops. Some accounts calculate that they have wreaked more agricultural damage than all the bombs of World War II. Their effect is so insidious that in 1930 the country of Borneo placed a bounty on them, offering payment for the adults and eggs; unfortunately, this was ineffective. Due to lack of natural enemies and to the aid of unwitting tourists, these animals have spread from their original homeland in Africa to Ceylon, Borneo, Japan, Hawaii, and Florida.

99. Thatcheria
Thatcheria mirabilis
MEANING: Respect
EXPLANATION: When the first Thatcheria specimen was discovered, scientists thought it was a freak of nature until many years later when more specimens like it were found. It is believed that the Thatcheria's structure inspired Frank Lloyd Wright to incorporate the spiral ramps in the design of the Guggenheim Art Museum in New York City. Wright's unique vision suffered the same reception as the first Thatcheria. Originally ridiculed by society, he eventually earned respect as the master architect of a building that is a work of art itself. This shell encourages recognition that seeking respect begins within. Treating oneself with respect signals acceptance of nothing less from others.

100. Elongated Tridacna Clam
Tridacna elongata
MEANING: Undeserving of a reputation; being misunderstood
EXPLANATION: This clam is a member of the Tridacna family. The largest tridacna, which can attain a weight of five hundred pounds, is aptly named the Giant Clam. Due to its imposing size, this same clam has also been dubbed the "man-eating clam." Capitalizing on the Giant Clam's four-foot girth, Hollywood created an undersea monster that traps men in its valves and devours them—which is pure fantasy. In reality, these gentle giants are vegetarians. In fact, because of their immense bulk, they are incapable of pursuing any meal, even plant life. To accommodate this, they grow algae within their bodies. Their skin contains transparent patches that allow the sun's rays to penetrate and provide photosynthesis for their gardens.

101. Pacific Trumpet Triton
Charonia tritonis
MEANING: One's purpose or calling in life
EXPLANATION: By cutting off the tip of the triton, one can blow into the shell and produce low tones resembling a loud trumpet. In Japan, shinto priests use these trumpets to call people in to pray.

102. Juno's Volute
Scaphella junonia
MEANING: Something hidden being exposed; truth being revealed
EXPLANATION: As is true with many material things in our society, the monetary value of shells is based on supply and demand. At one time, Juno's Volute shells were rare and,

consequently, quite expensive. They are now easily affordable because hidden beds of them have been exposed. (See no. 106, Torr's Whelk, for a shell that has taken the opposite direction in value.)

103. Melon Baler Volute
Melo melo
MEANING: Needing to bail out of a situation
EXPLANATION: These shells are found in territories where the native people transport themselves in canoes. If the canoe takes on too much water, the volute shells are employed as buckets to bail out the canoe and prevent it from sinking. This use is so prevalent that the shells are called baler volutes.

104. Precious Wentletrap
Epitonium scalare
MEANING: Con man; fraud; deceit
EXPLANATION: In the 1800s, this shell was extremely rare and fetched large sums of money. Some people in China decided to capitalize on this by creating rice-paste counterfeits that were sold as the genuine shell. The eventual discovery of large beds of Wentletraps devalued the shell, ending this fraudulent practice. *Note:* This shell will usually indicate an acquaintance but may also refer to deceit of oneself.

105. Lightning Whelk
Busycon contrarium
MEANING: Inspiration
EXPLANATION: The Lightning Whelk obtains its name from the jagged lightning-bolt pattern on its shell. Lightning has classically been a symbol of enlightenment, as when it appears above someone's head in a drawing. As discussed with no. 71, Indian Chank, Hindus consider the rare left-

handed chank shell to be sacred. This form of the shell is very scarce, as it occurs only through mutation. One source estimates that the left-handed version appears in one out of every 6.25 million chanks. (See no. 79, Marble Cone, for a discussion of left-handedness.) Almost every univalve follows a growth pattern spiraling in a clockwise direction, ultimately yielding an opening on the right side. One very unusual exception to this growth pattern is found in the Lightning Whelk. This shell naturally grows in a counterclockwise direction and, as you can see in this photograph, opens on the left side. When people in the United States learned of the value of left-handed shells in India, they were inspired to export Lightning Whelks, which were warmly received. In my practice, I enjoy handing out "inspiration" shells to my clients. Lightning Whelk shells wash up on the shore in Florida, but living in Massachusetts, I am reduced to shopping for my supply of them. Once when I visited a local shell store to replenish my inventory, the storeowner informed me that he had sold out of them as quickly as they arrived because people from India had bought them all. Although I failed in my mission, there was consolation in being an eyewitness to the success of this inspired connection of the left-handed whelks to the sacred chank shell.

106. Torr's Whelk
Godfreyna torri
MEANING: Someone or something increasing in value
EXPLANATION: Once plentiful and inexpensive, this whelk is now banned from collection due to its scarcity. (See no. 102, Juno's Volute, for the reverse situation.) Its new status has multiplied the value of any Torr's Whelk already in one's possession. This shell indicates a circumstance where a friend may become a lover or an object may acquire more value than previously realized. Someone, or something, becomes more precious to you.

Name and Appearance Group

107. Donkey Ear Abalone
Haliotis asinina
MEANING: A foolish or asinine request
EXPLANATION: The scientific name for this shell is
Haliotis asinina.

108. Golden-brown Ancilla
Ancillista velesiana
MEANING: Being taken for granted; being treated
like slave labor; being unappreciated
EXPLANATION: In Latin, *ancilla* means "maidservant."

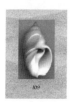

109. Lienard's Ancilla
Ancilla lienardi
MEANING: Being appreciated for one's services
EXPLANATION: This is another possibility of one's
attitude toward another's service.

110. Cut-Ribbed Ark
Andara floridana
MEANING: Rescue, safety
EXPLANATION: In the Bible story, Noah's Ark was the
vessel that saved every living species from extinction.

111. Turkey Wing Ark
Arca zebra

MEANING: Unhealthy behavior that must come to an end immediately

EXPLANATION: At times, stopping "cold turkey" is the best approach, as a gradual weaning process will prolong the time spent engaging in the damaging behavior.

112. Perforated Auger
Terebra pertusa

MEANING: Holes or weak spots in one's argument; errors; flaws

EXPLANATION: When an object is perforated, it is punctured with holes.

113. Cancellate Beak-Shell
Varicospira cancellata

MEANING: All the nagging "shoulds" in life

EXPLANATION: The hard beak of a bird is used to peck at food. When a person is henpecked, someone is urging or nagging him or her to do something.

114. Necklace Cerith
Clypeomorus moniliferus

MEANING: A healthy ego

EXPLANATION: In some texts, ceriths are called horn shells, evoking the expression "Toot your own horn," as with someone who clearly acknowledges his or her own strengths. *Note:* Disliking this shell indicates an overdeveloped ego that may be perceived as bragging or boastful.

115. Squamose Chiton (partial underside view)
Chiton squamosus
MEANING: Self-abuse; unhealthy behaviors; addictions
EXPLANATION: This photograph shows a portion of
a chiton—four of its plates viewed from underneath.
Chiton shells are constructed from eight separate
overlapping plates, and they bear a resemblance to the protective
suits of armor worn by knights of old. Accordingly, chitons are
often called coat-of-mail shells. Addictions are some people's way
of shielding themselves. Whether drugs, alcohol, food, sex, shopping, or gambling, all addictions serve as unhealthy methods of
self-medication for defending against life's pain. Attraction to
this shell may refer to the person who chooses it or to someone in
his or her experience.

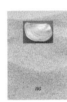

116. Pandora Clam
Pandora gouldiana
MEANING: Curiosity; the possibility of a curious
nature leading to trouble
EXPLANATION: According to mythology, Pandora
was the person whose curiosity caused her to open a
box that unleashed all the ills in the world.

117. Hieroglyphic Venus Clam
Lioconcha hieroglyphica
MEANING: The key to understanding; making a
breakthrough
EXPLANATION: Hieroglyphic, the ancient Egyptian
pictorial script, was indecipherable until the discovery of the Rosetta stone. The Rosetta stone contained the same message in several languages, one of which was hieroglyphic. With this

key to decoding hieroglyphic, we have obtained a wealth of insight and understanding regarding an important chapter in the history of mankind.

118. Prostitute Venus Clam
Pitar lupanaria
MEANING: Going through the motions; action without heart behind it
EXPLANATION: A prostitute exchanges sex for money or security. In this relationship, sex, which should be united with love, has been reduced to barter, and heartfelt emotions do not apply.

119. Wedding Cake Venus Clam
Callanaitis disjecta
MEANING: Wedding, marriage, committed relationship
EXPLANATION: The tiers of these shells suggest a wedding cake, such as those traditionally served on one's wedding day as part of the festivities. *Note:* This can also refer to long-term relationships that aren't formalized through marriage.

120. Blood Mouth Conch
Strombus luhuanus
MEANING: Good and bad news; victory after struggle
EXPLANATION: A bloody mouth is indicative of the fact that someone was involved in a fight. This scenario may be likened to someone who arrives with a bloody mouth and says, "If you think I look bad, you should see the other guy."

121. Butterfly Conch
Strombus pipus
MEANING: Underestimating; devaluing
EXPLANATION: The butterfly emerges as a metamorphosis of the caterpillar. Some people are unable to see their own potential and identify themselves as caterpillars, never realizing the beauty they hold inside.

122. Hawkwing Conch
Strombus raninus
MEANING: Being extremely observant; allowing nothing to get past one
EXPLANATION: In the animal kingdom, hawks are noted for their keen eyesight. Recognizing this, we refer to a highly observant person as someone who has the eyes of a hawk.

123. Rooster Tail Conch
Strombus gallus
MEANING: Needing to wake up; receiving a wake-up call
EXPLANATION: The rooster crowing, signaling dawn, is nature's alarm clock.

124. Admirable Cone
Conus praecellens
MEANING: An admirable person
EXPLANATION: This shell represents admirable qualities in oneself or one's perception of others. Sometimes it's easier to notice the less-appealing qualities shared with others than the positive aspects. It may be less obvious, but we often share the positive, highly regarded qualities as well.

125. Alphabet Cone
Conus spurius

MEANING: Needing to master the fundamentals before proceeding; tendency to skip steps

EXPLANATION: As young children, we are taught the alphabet. This essential tool eventually enables us to communicate with each other through reading and writing. Every letter of the alphabet is equally important; skipping any of them will make reading impossible. This shell may appeal to someone who habitually begins assembling a new product without reading the directions, determined to reach goals quickly and often suffering as a consequence. It addresses the importance of laying a strong foundation to ensure success—one step at a time.

126. Governor's Cone
Conus gubernator

MEANING: A dangerous leader ignoring the opinions and feelings of others; the importance of thinking for oneself

EXPLANATION: A governor is always a person with power over others; the governor holds the highest office of elected leadership in a state. As noted with no. 76, Geography Cone, cone shells are poisonous, indicating danger. Combined, these facts indicate that the Governor's Cone concerns a dangerous leader. Such a leader may not honor the opinions or feelings of those under him or her but is motivated by the power of having followers. Followers are expected to abdicate their own thoughts in order to obey the leader unquestionably. In extreme situations, there may be indoctrination through brainwashing. This shell cautions those who choose it to think for themselves.

127. Illustrious Cone
Conus excelsus
MEANING: Being famous and celebrated; achieving praise and recognition
EXPLANATION: *Illustrious* can be defined as "famous, celebrated, and renowned," indicating that a person attracted to this shell might expect honor or acclaim.

128. Leopard Cone
Conus leopardus
MEANING: Trying to fit in rather than risking being considered different
EXPLANATION: As in the adage "A leopard can't change its spots," this shell suggests that people ultimately return to their true natures no matter how much they try to pretend otherwise.

129. Rose Coral
MEANING: Listening to one's head; analyzing everything before taking action
EXPLANATION: Although this is Rose Coral, its appearance resembles its close relative, brain coral. The person attracted to this coral thinks before acting. Logic takes precedence over emotion. In the extreme, this person may analyze everything to the point of inaction due to "paralysis of the analysis."

130. Chick Pea Cowrie
Cypraea mauiensis
MEANING: Being extremely sensitive and easily hurt
EXPLANATION: In the children's fairy tale of the princess and the pea, the pea is used as a measure of sensitivity. The princess is so sensitive that she can

detect its presence even when the pea is buried beneath a stack of mattresses.

131. Warted Egg Cowrie
Calpurnus verrucosus

MEANING: Needing to detach; cutting the umbilical cord; gaining independence

EXPLANATION: Another common name for this shell is the Umbilical Ovula. The umbilical cord connects a baby to its mother while in her womb. This cord is severed at birth, allowing the baby and mother to become two separate units. This is the source of a figure of speech referring to someone needing to cut the umbilical cord if too dependent on another. This person may feel incapable and lack self-reliance, simply because he or she has had another decide everything. Having no experience at making decisions can make a person feel inept and unsure. Selecting this shell indicates the need for independence to strengthen one's sense of self-sufficiency.

132. Granulated Cowrie
Cypraea granulata

MEANING: Being falsely sweet; having ulterior motives

EXPLANATION: Granulated sugar is used to sweeten. In human behavior, this is likened to an overly sweet person who may be manipulating others for personal benefit.

133. Map Cowrie
Cypraea mappa

MEANING: Needing to review one's map of beliefs

EXPLANATION: This shell indicates that it's time to review beliefs in order to identify those that may be limiting experience rather than adding to it.

134. Sieve Cowrie
Cypraea cribraria
MEANING: Being forgetful; possibly being con-
cerned about appearing unintelligent
EXPLANATION: When people find that they can't
seem to retain information, they use the expression
"My mind is like a sieve."

135. West Indian Cup and Saucer
Crucibulum auricula
MEANING: A party, celebration, social event
EXPLANATION: This shell resembles a miniature
cup-and-saucer set. The diminutive scale is reminis-
cent of those used for a child's tea party.

136. Common Distorsio
Distorsio anus
MEANING: Someone distorting the truth; being a liar
EXPLANATION: This shell received its name from the
distorted, mangled growth pattern around its mouth.
When something is distorted, it is twisted or
stretched into an irregular form. A person who distorts the truth
stretches it or lies. *Note:* While this usually shows up as someone in
the person's life, it can also represent a person who subconsciously
thinks "everybody lies," which he or she then uses as "permission"
to lie as well.

137. Common Frog Shell
Bursa rana
MEANING: Finding the wrong partner—not your
prince charming
EXPLANATION: In fairy tales, the bewitched prince
turns into a frog. It takes a princess willing to kiss

this frog to restore the prince to his former self. From this popular theme comes the expression "You have to kiss a lot of frogs before you find your prince." This shell is the Common Frog Shell, which remains a frog, whereas the next shell—the Noble Frog Shell—is the prince.

138. Noble Frog Shell
Bursa margaritula
MEANING: Finding the ideal partner—your prince charming
EXPLANATION: See no. 137.

139. Leafy Jewel Box
Chama macerophylla
MEANING: Testing one's values; having the courage of one's convictions
EXPLANATION: A jewel box is for storing valued possessions. However, this shell addresses inner values rather than material objects. This shell also indicates that one's morals and values may be challenged.

140. Belcher's Latirus
Latirus belcheri
MEANING: Seeking forgiveness
EXPLANATION: In many societies, people ask to be pardoned when they let gas escape in a noisy belch.
Note: It is possible that those attracted to this shell may most need to forgive themselves; people sometimes believe they deserve punishment for something and unconsciously keep themselves in unhealthy situations.

141. Squat Latirus
Latirus tumens
MEANING: Needing to forgive others; needing to let go of a grudge
EXPLANATION: Squatting is a posture that compresses our body and lowers our center of gravity. This allows us to bear greater weight than would be possible while standing erect. Weight lifters employ this stance when picking up heavy barbells. Holding a grudge can create a heavy, debilitating burden; letting go of one can be liberating, as if a great weight has been released. *Note:* For some, blaming others for their unhappiness can be a great burden that results in self-sabotage. Ironically, they dare not be successful if this would let the other person off the hook. They prefer to hold the other person accountable for their ruined life and are thus trapped in a need to fail.

142. Volcano Limpet
Diodora aspera
MEANING: Needing to relieve tension before things explode
EXPLANATION: Active volcanoes provide Mother Earth with a natural venting system to release the pressurized contents of her core. A similar need arises in people's lives, indicating a need for relief from building pressure.

143. Episcopal Miter
Mitra mitra
MEANING: Religion or spiritual values
EXPLANATION: This shell obtained its name from the resemblance to the miter headgear worn by clergy. Attraction to this shell encourages a more conscious evaluation of one's religious or spiritual values.

144. Pontifical Miter
Mitra stictica
MEANING: Mediating for peace; seeking harmony
EXPLANATION: In the Catholic religion, the pope personifies God's emissary trying to establish peace on Earth.

145. Queen Miter
Vexillum regina
MEANING: A boss or superior; someone acting superior or bossy
EXPLANATION: A queen is the supreme female authority of her territory. Those acting queen-like expect others to bow to their dictates.

146. Scarlet Miter
Vexillum coccineum
MEANING: Embarrassment, humiliation, shame
EXPLANATION: Scarlet is associated with a person's embarrassment, as when someone blushes red. In the classic novel *The Scarlet Letter*, Nathaniel Hawthorne used the scarlet letter *A* as a symbol for adultery to be worn as an emblem broadcasting one's shame.

147. Mangrove Murex
Chicoreus capucinus
MEANING: Feeling overburdened and swamped
EXPLANATION: Mangrove trees grow in swampy waters. Someone swamped with work is buried under a mound of obligations.

148. Saul's Murex
Chicoreus saulii

MEANING: Outside advisor, therapist, counselor

EXPLANATION: Saul was the first king of Israel at a time when all disputes were settled by appealing to the king. His grandson, King Solomon, was famous for his wisdom when dispensing advice.

149. Snipe's Bill Murex
Murex haustellum

MEANING: Mean-spiritedness; negative comments designed to lower someone's stature; gossip

EXPLANATION: Hidden from view, snipers shoot at unsuspecting people. Instead of bullets, some people employ criticism to the same end. Their words are potshots capable of wounding and destroying other people's spirits just as bullets destroy the body. *Note:* While this most often refers to an acquaintance, it's also possible that the person who picks this shell should examine his or her own beliefs about sniping.

150. Venus Comb Murex
Murex pecten

MEANING: Healthy self-centeredness; self-love; focusing on one's needs; discovering and living one's truth

EXPLANATION: The comb symbolizes vanity or absorption with the self, as in those people who fuss over their hair. This shell indicates a desire to take care of, and pursue, one's own needs. *Note:* Disliking this shell may indicate someone who is focused on everyone else's needs while paying no attention to his or her own. While the word *selfish* has negative connotations, disliking this shell reveals an uneasy feeling that one may end up drained by those who constantly require attention. It's important not to get so depleted attending to others that a person has no energy available for him or herself. This shell, more than any other, teaches how we love. People often think that if they are not selfish, they will be loved; however, under those circumstances when someone does tell them they are loved, they are not fulfilled because the person doesn't truly know them. They have spent too much time addressing everybody else's needs, which leaves no time for self-exploration. Those who like this shell have allowed themselves time to discover and live their truth. So when they hear someone say "I love you," they can feel it all the way to their soul, because the person is responding to their authentic self, not to some projected image.

151. Common Nutmeg
Cancellaria reticulata
MEANING: Seeking more adventure; desiring to add spice to one's life
EXPLANATION: Nutmeg is a spice used to enhance the flavor of food.

152. Cat's Tongue Oyster
Spondylus linguaefelis
MEANING: Keeping silent; not speaking up
EXPLANATION: The expression "Cat got your tongue" refers to someone who is tongue-tied and remains silent.

153. Nude Thorny Oyster
Spondylus anacanthus
MEANING: Being someone who speaks the truth and shatters illusions; being comfortable in one's skin
EXPLANATION: The person picking this shell holds no illusions and is comfortable embracing the naked, unembellished truth. Less-secure individuals may not welcome the

shattering of their illusions, so the truth should be spoken with caution. *Note:* This most often refers to the person who picks the shell, though it may also reflect someone in his or her experience.

154. Eye of Judas Purpura
Purpura planospira

MEANING: Betrayal; lack of loyalty

EXPLANATION: In the New Testament, Judas betrayed Jesus, and it has been suggested that this act was necessary for Jesus to fulfill his destiny. The lesson of this shell is that no matter what other people appear to do to us, we are allowing it or creating it on some level—even something that we would not consciously say we want. This shell offers solace by suggesting that even when one has been betrayed, eventually a purpose will be revealed. In the grander scheme of life, it may lead one to new avenues of discovery.

155. Paper Moon Scallop
Amusium papyraceum

MEANING: Books, scholarship, school, study

EXPLANATION: The Latin name for this shell is *papyraceum*. In antiquity, the papyrus plant was used as a source for making paper. This shell may refer to school, or it may be advising detailed study of a situation.

156. Apple Snail
Pomacea paludosa

MEANING: Losing innocence; confronting reality

EXPLANATION: In the Bible, after eating fruit from the forbidden tree of knowledge, Adam and Eve's innocent state in Eden's paradise was lost forever. Becoming aware of their naked bodies, they felt shame for the first time. *Note:* Loss of naïveté is often accompanied by emotional pain. It can hurt to discover that the world is not as previously believed.

157. Ram's Horn
Marisa cornuarietis
MEANING: Forcing one's opinion on others
EXPLANATION: In nature, rams forcefully butt heads trying to dominate each other.

158. Triumphant Star
Guildfordia triumphans
MEANING: Victory, triumph
EXPLANATION: The word *triumphant* means "victorious, conquering, successful."

159. Giant Sundial
Architectonica maxima
MEANING: Patience
EXPLANATION: Sundials were an early method used to track the slow, steady passage of time.

160. Tadpole Triton
Gyrineum gyrinum
MEANING: Young person, child
EXPLANATION: A tadpole is the immature stage in the development of a frog. *Note:* Depending on the other shells in the arrangement, this triton may refer either to a child in someone's life or the person's feelings toward children.

161. Solander's Trivia
Trivia solandri
MEANING: Trivial, unimportant
EXPLANATION: By definition, trivia is considered of little importance. Attraction to this shell may indicate a belief that everything in life is of little consequence. Desires are downplayed or squashed completely to avoid the pain of discovering that those desires might not be valued by others. *Note:* Disliking this shell indicates a belief that nothing is unimportant, that every detail deserves consideration, that any desire is worthy of exploration—and this person would not appreciate being informed otherwise.

162. Grinning Tun
Malea ringens
MEANING: Grinning; smiling; maintaining a sense of humor
EXPLANATION: The act of smiling or grinning can create good feelings within, making any situation easier to tolerate. We are given the choice to look at the world as either an optimist or a pessimist, and this shell reminds us of the value of maintaining good humor. *Note:* If someone dislikes this shell, it is an indication that this person has difficulty maintaining a cheery disposition. This might indicate a situation in which someone has a great need to be taken seriously, and joking or making light of the situation may be counterproductive.

163. Pencil Urchin
MEANING: Communication; the importance of sharing thoughts and feelings
EXPLANATION: A pencil is a writing implement used to express our thoughts.

164. Sherbet Urchin
MEANING: Paying attention to one's diet, particularly regarding proper nutrition and vitamins
EXPLANATION: For those concerned with the nutritional content of their diet, sherbet offers a lower-fat substitute for ice cream. By extension, this urchin refers to healthy eating habits.

165. Tuxedo Urchin
MEANING: Being polished and tactful
EXPLANATION: Tuxedos are formal wear designed for occasions where one wishes to make a good impression. They lend a polished look to one's appearance and a dignity to the event. Attraction to this urchin indicates a person who opts to cushion words in an effort to make difficult statements more palatable.

166. Elephant Snout Volute
Cymbium glans
MEANING: Nostalgia; memories; being held hostage to the past
EXPLANATION: As in the saying "An elephant never forgets," this shell will hold an attraction for people frozen in time, either from longing for the good old days and clinging to one's glory days or from wondering "what if?" things had been different or "if only" they had made different choices. Either way, such people may be stunted in their growth process, unable to recognize and enjoy the blessings of today. This shell is a reminder that one should not allow the past to define or limit experience. *Note:* Disliking this shell indicates a desire to escape the past and create a new identity.

167. Shuttlecock Volva
Volva volva
MEANING: Being pulled in two directions; being caught in a triangular relationship; equating love to quality time

EXPLANATION: In the game of badminton, the shuttlecock is batted back and forth across a net. It no sooner arrives on one side than it is hit back to the other. When this movement in two directions occurs in relationships, it can be very uncomfortable. It may require a difficult choice as to where, or with whom, one's support, attention, or love will dwell. The "where" may take the form of one person choosing between another and other desires such as work, hobbies, and friends. "With whom" may express itself as a triangular relationship with two people battling for the attention of the third. They may find that triangles take the form of competition in other arenas, such as at work or with friends, where there is an opportunity to be chosen over a co-worker for some project or to be singled out as someone's best friend. A person selecting this shell may be on any point of the triangle. Most often they are the one needing to be chosen, which they then interpret as evidence that they are loved, but they may also experience being the one pulled in two directions, demonstrating their love for another. *Note:* To feel loved, people attracted to this shell need proof, and action—in the form of being chosen—speaks louder than words. An underlying need of "proof" of someone's affection may cause them to become constantly involved in triangles as a pattern in life. Each triangle provides them with another opportunity to be the one chosen, to have someone's actions say, "I choose to be with you over any other alternative." When this occurs, they have gained that highly prized quality time—a demonstration of love which mere words could not convey.

168. Watering Pot
Brechites attrahens
MEANING: Reaping what is sown; taking responsibility for one's own actions
EXPLANATION: Yes, this is a shell. In fact, it is classed as a bivalve. The arrow in this photograph indicates the two halves of the bivalve where the animal begins life. (See page xii for the definition of *bivalves*.) It then proceeds to form a long tube containing tiny perforations at the top. Water emerges through these holes in a spray formation, much like a watering can—hence its name. We use watering pots to dispense the life-sustaining water that plants need for growth. Careful attention determines the condition of each plant; one must be cautious to neither overwater nor underwater seedlings, or they will not survive. In similar fashion, people are responsible for the consequences of any actions they take in life. *Note:* People who dislike this shell may not want to take responsibility for their actions. Sometimes it feels safer to follow orders and be able to blame others should failure occur. This person may not experience much success, because ensuring a fallback position of placing blame indicates an expectation of failure. However, allowing another to make decisions still leaves one responsible for the choice to give away one's personal power.

Intuition Group

169. Bear's Paw
Hippopus hippopus
MEANING: Being nurturing; being an affectionate, nature-loving individual
Note: The person picking this shell would mother everybody if possible. This is the person who can be counted on to provide hugs—the proverbial Earth Mother, though it may apply to either a man or a woman with nurturing qualities.

170. Little Star Bolma
Bolma asteriola
MEANING: Having great potential; setting high goals for oneself
Note: Disliking this shell indicates a desire to hide one's potential, thereby eliminating expectations from others. This person may "play dumb," or "lower the bar," to keep true talents and abilities well hidden. Accepting tasks for which one is overqualified guarantees no failures, resulting in a safe life but not a very fulfilling one.

171. Angaria Delphinula
Angaria delphinus
MEANING: Arguments, anger

172. Aculeate Delphinula
Angaria aculeata
MEANING: Regretting something said—as in the expression "Open mouth, insert foot"—or unsaid

173. Purple Pacific Drupe
Drupa morum
MEANING: Depression, possibly requiring therapy

174. Fossil
Fossil Cephalopod
MEANING: Vindication; being proven right (perhaps after a long wait)

Note: Attraction to this shell challenges one to explore one's hidden beliefs that require vindication. With this shell, the need to be right supersedes all else, and any expectations that manifest, whether positive or negative, are received with equal joy if they allow verification of a subconscious belief. This need to be right can be combined with any belief to a strong effect. For example, if self-esteem is tied to being acknowledged as correct, it can be safer for those who believe that nothing works out for them to fail than to succeed. This way, every time they fail, a hidden part of them can privately rejoice because they were right. However, this is just one example of a type of belief; this shell is not about failure but about verifying whatever belief is held as correct. People holding limiting beliefs have two possible solutions: one choice is to allow themselves to be wrong without taking it as a failure; a second choice is to change the thing they have to be right about. They can just as easily believe they will always succeed, for example, and through this create circumstances to be right about that belief. The desire to be right about everything may entail constant devotion to study so that all questions can be answered. Disliking this fossil reveals the limitations that this habit places on one's time. The inner self is suggesting that the need to be right has become a trap that is diminishing the quality of life. Regarding inner knowledge, if this shell is disliked, it may indicate a past experience when it would have been preferable to be wrong rather than to have those worst suspicions confirmed. Such people may actually shun, or turn off, any intuitive feelings at all. They are not trying to avoid being wrong; they are trying to avoid knowledge which can carry pain. For example, suppose you knew intuitively that your best friend's husband was cheating on her. You would wish with all your heart that you were wrong. You have no desire to be proven right. And the pain of this could cause you to turn off your intuition rather than know such things. People actively pursuing a spiritual path need to resolve this feeling if they are to gain more knowledge.

175. Polynesian Harp
Harpa gracilis
MEANING: Skill or mastery of a craft

176. Bullmouth Helmet
Cypraecassis rufa
MEANING: Someone who is capable and well-suited to the task
Note: This can refer to acquaintances, but ultimately it refers to an issue with the person who chooses the shell.

177. Victor Dan's Latiaxis
Mipus vicdani
MEANING: Love of pets and animals

178. Nigrite Murex
Hexaplex nigritus
MEANING: Courage to overcome negative emotions such as anger and depression

179. Foliated Thorn Murex
Ceratostoma foliata
MEANING: Official forms, contracts, legal documents

180. New England Neptune
Neptunea lyrata
MEANING: Being very uncomfortable with oneself; wanting to escape a situation; possibly wanting off the planet
Note: In extreme situations, this person may seek escape using drugs or alcohol or may even consider suicide.

181. Bleeding Tooth Nerite
Nerita peloronta
MEANING: Sudden change in circumstances leaving one unprepared

182. Gibbous Olive
Olivancillaria gibbosa
MEANING: Being a copycat; desiring to do something just to keep up with someone else; fear of being left behind or ridiculed

183. Tent Olive
Oliva porphyria
MEANING: Low self-esteem; low self-worth; tendency to settle for less
Note: This person has a tendency to settle for less rather than aspire to anything more due to the feeling that he or she doesn't deserve any better. For example, in an unhappy relationship, this person would be grateful to be in any relationship at all and not expect to deserve happiness. At work, this person would be thinking, "At least I am employed," and not expect it to be fulfilling.

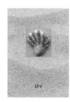

184. Kitten's Paw Oyster
Plicatula gibbosa
MEANING: Unconditional love
Note: When practicing unconditional love, people sometimes forget to also unconditionally love themselves. Also, it is possible to love people without loving their behavior.

185. Most Graceful Pagoda
Columbarium formosissimum
MEANING: Grace under pressure
Note: Attraction to this shell indicates a positive choice regarding how one responds to tense moments. This person values the ability to remain calm in the midst of the storm. The challenge is to exhibit composure when others might become hysterical. This person may experience many pressure-filled situations in life as training opportunities in grace.

186. Muricate Purpura
Neorapana muricata
MEANING: Recognizing that limitations are of one's own making
Note: Elephants are massive animals, yet they allow their movements to be restricted when enclosed in a fence only a few inches high. They could crush the fence with no effort, but because they consider themselves fenced in, they behave accordingly. Attraction to this shell indicates those who imprison themselves unnecessarily and would be well-advised to get out of their own way.

187. Sea Biscuit
MEANING: Pride; being concerned about other people's perceptions of oneself; craving external validation
Note: Pride is all about others' perceptions, so the person picking this shell may be relying on other people's feedback to determine self-worth. This person's thoughts and behaviors are carefully orchestrated to elicit proof that he or she deserves love, and nothing is said which might jeopardize that. Such a person may succeed in maintaining a balance on someone's pedestal, but at the price of self-respect. There may come a time when he or she must decide, "Do I care more if *you* like me, or if *I* like me?"

188. Cinnamon Roll Snail
Euhadra
MEANING: Entitlement; recognizing one's own rights

189. Telescope Snail
Telescopium telescopium
MEANING: Remaining in the background; being out of sight; inspiring others without recognition
Note: This shell teaches us the need to distinguish between the desire to heal a situation and the need to take credit for the healing. The person selecting the Telescope Snail may find that approaching someone with direct advice will meet with resistance. The lesson is to plant the seeds of an idea while remaining in the background, which allows the other person to keep ownership of the idea. Such a person will unknowingly act on one's advice but without giving credit for it.

190. Tropidophora Land Snail
Tropidophora deliciosa
MEANING: Feeling that nothing comes easily; progress through struggle
Note: The person selecting this shell may lead a life of struggle in which nothing is handed over easily. Attraction to this shell reveals a person who probably would not value anything that came too easily. Ascending the mountain, we can be chauffeured in style or claw our way through the back trails on foot. This person would not appreciate the view unless arriving scraped and bruised from the arduous climb.

191. Orange Spider Conch
Lambis crocata crocata
MEANING: Changing roles or jobs, or change within a job

192. Violet Spider Conch
Lambis violacea
MEANING: Temptation and discernment
Note: Temptation will test where a person's true values lie. It also may distract from what is truly beneficial or satisfying in life. Desires can manifest easily, but this shell serves as a reminder that goals may fall short of providing fulfillment. This teaches discriminating between what the personality may desire and what fills the soul. As each attained goal fails to provide happiness, one's definition of what is tempting may become more discerning. Temptations can ultimately serve as distractions from much more beneficial pursuits.

193. Long-Spined Star
Astraea phoebia
MEANING: Confronting one's destiny
Note: People attracted to this shell may be keenly aware that they are here for a mission of some sort, and they may even know what it is. However, they might not welcome the roles they are required to play. Perceiving the path as difficult, they may avoid choices that bring them closer to fulfilling their destinies.

194. Candelabra Trophon
Boreotrophon candelabrum
MEANING: Burning the candle at both ends; taking on too many projects
Note: Attraction to this shell cautions that scattering one's energy in too many directions may result in ineffectiveness.

195. Banded Tun
Tonna sulcosa
MEANING: Needing to accept the things we can't change, changing the things we can, and recognizing the difference
Note: This mirrors the "serenity prayer" popular in rehabilitation programs. Attraction to this shell often indicates that someone is accepting something which could be changed or trying to change something which is not within that person's control.

196. South African Turban
Turbo sarmaticus
MEANING: Peeling away the outer layers to find inner light
Note: This shell teaches us to shed the beliefs we have stored regarding who we are based on other people's or society's dictates. By ignoring these impositions, we can shed false or influenced concepts of ourselves and dig down to find individual truth.

197. Boar's Tusk
Dentalium aprinum
MEANING: Dullness; lack of excitement; the safety of routine
Note: Disliking this shell indicates that one's behavior may be predicated on the desire to avoid boredom.

198. Flinder's Vase
Altivasum flindersi
MEANING: Frustration; stifled creativity; knowing there is more to life

Note: The person selecting this shell may ask, "Is that all there is?" sensing that there is more to life and his or her identity. However, attempts to find it may be frustrating.

199. Bednall's Volute
Volutoconus bednalli
MEANING: Networking; connections
Note: Networking involves partnering with others. Together, these connections form a whole that is greater than the sum of its parts. This shell refers to connections on many levels. It is about reaching out to others, joining forces, and discovering that even seemingly unrelated or distant things are connected.

200. Hunter's Volute
Cymbiolista hunteri
MEANING: Hunting; stalking; signs of obsession

Further Shell Study
I conduct several educational seminars that may be customized for length and age-appropriateness. These seminars employ hands-on interaction with shells from all over the world as well as overhead-projector images of the mollusks. In addition to showing the shells' natural beauty, pictures enable you to gain an appreciation for the beauty of the colors and patterns displayed on the mollusks' bodies. This photographic evidence also enhances our comprehension of the animals' intelligence. In these seminars, you will be able to feel the polished surface of a cowrie and hold the paper-light nautilus cradle in your hands. Through the images, you will see the female

nautilus in her cradle as well as view the janthina floating on its self-constructed raft. You will have a front-row seat as you witness a cone injecting its poison or watch the vampires and heroes in action.

"Friends from the Sea" is based on the science of the shells and mollusks. This seminar is popular with children as well as adults. We will discuss the five classes of mollusks in terms of their anatomy and behaviors. We will also learn how shells have interacted with man throughout history. Since many shells are named for their appearance, we will participate in an exercise to see if we can match shells to their names. This seminar focuses on the shells found in the Behavior, Interaction, and Name and Appearance groups.

"The Language of Seashells I" covers information similar to that in "Friends from the Sea," but it takes it one step further. Using the names of the shells as well as the mollusks' anatomy, behaviors, and interaction with man, we discuss the derivation of the meanings assigned to each shell. We also add shells in the Intuition group and shells not included in *Ocean Oracle*.

"The Language of Seashells II" explores the divination aspects in greater depth. It includes the information in "The Language of Seashells I" and builds on the metaphysical components. The workshop includes personal instruction by the author in obtaining your own shell-divination messages.

The author welcomes questions regarding shells, mollusks, or this method of divination.

Contact the author at (978) 840-4357 or visit *www.oceanoracle.com* for answers or for information on training as a seashell reader.